Reading Poetry

Peter Robinson was born in Salford, Lancashire, in 1953 and grew up mainly in Liverpool. He has degrees from the universities of York and Cambridge. After teaching for many years in Japan, he returned to Europe in 2007 and is currently Professor of English and American Literature at the University of Reading. The poetry editor for Two Rivers Press, author of many books of poetry, translations, prose, and literary criticism, he is married with two daughters.

Reading Poetry
an anthology

edited by Peter Robinson
illustrated by Sally Castle

TWO
RIVERS
PRESS

First published in the UK in 2011 by Two Rivers Press
7 DENMARK ROAD, READING RG1 5PA
www.tworiverspress.com

ISBN 978-1-901677-72-0

British Library Cataloguing in Publication Data. A catalogue record for this book
is available from the British Library.

Two Rivers Press is represented in the UK by Inpress Ltd
and distributed by Central Books Ltd.

Cover design and illustrations by Sally Castle
Text design by Nadja Guggi and typeset in Janson and Parisine

Printed and bound in Great Britain by CPI Antony Rowe, Chippenham & Eastbourne.

Acknowledgements
The poems in this anthology are reproduced with the permission of their copyright
holders, the individual poets for poems previously uncollected, and Two Rivers Press
for poems from Adrian Blamires, *The Effect of Coastal Processes* (2005) and *The Pang
Valley* (2010); Jane Draycott, *Tideway* (2002); John Froy, *Eggshell: A Decorator's Notes*
(2007); A. F. Harrold, *Flood* (2009); Gill Learner, *The Agister's Experiment* (2011);
Victoria Pugh, *Mrs Marvellous* (2008); Peter Robinson, *English Nettles and Other Poems*
(2010); Lesley Saunders, *Her Leafy Eye* (2009); and Susan Utting, *Houses Without Walls*
(2006). Two Rivers Press would like to thank their publishers for kind permission
to reprint poems from the following collections: Jane Draycott, *Prince Rupert's Drop*
(OUP/Carcanet Press, 1999), *The Night Tree* (Carcanet Press, 2004) and *Over* (Carcanet
Press, 2009); Wendy Klein, *Cuba in the Blood* (Cinnamon Press, 2009); Lesley Saunders,
No Doves (Mulfran Press, 2010); and Susan Utting, *Striptease* (Smith/Doorstop 2001).

Contents

Introduction

Among the many things that surprised me when I returned to England, to live in Reading, after almost two decades working in Japan, was that the town had a thriving poetry scene. That I didn't expect this might be yet another instance of its being much maligned. There was at least one reason why I should have been prepared to think differently. In 2005, at a bookshop chain opposite the old Speke Airport in Liverpool, I picked out from the shelves a very well designed and produced book, *The Effect of Coastal Processes*, by a poet I'd never heard of called Adrian Blamires. The publisher's name was Two Rivers Press, again new to me, and I could have noted, but didn't, that they were based in Reading.

Still, it can't have been long after I arrived in the town that not only did I somehow recall that the largest archive of one of my favourite English poets, Bernard Spencer, was held at the university where I was now employed, but also that there was a small press that produced beautifully designed editions based in the town. I attempted to make contact with the press, and, seeing that some of its poets were due to read at the first Henley Literary Festival, I went along, heard Adrian read for the first time, met Jane Draycott, who introduced the reading, and John Froy, the press's then co-ordinator. I also bought a sheaf of their books.

At about the same time I discovered the existence of a Poets' Café, which met once a month at the old labour exchange, now an arts centre, in South Street. Though suspicious of open mic sets in which anyone could step up and read whatever they might think a poem, I was again surprised to discover that not only did many of the poets who read have collections to their names, some published by Two Rivers Press, others from a variety of different outfits, small and less so, but there were very few poems read that refused to return an echo, and hardly any that elicited a wince of empathetic embarrassment on my part.

The Poets' Café was and is hosted by another Two Rivers poet whose work I didn't know before coming to the town, one who managed the social transitions between heterogeneous readers with an enviably witty improvisational skill, and matched it with similarly impressive ice-breaking poems: this was Ashley Harrold. What's more, when I first arrived, there was still a flourishing continuing education department at the university, which employed Susan Utting, another Two Rivers poet, as its poetry tutor. She, I discovered, had not only set up the Poets' Café, but had long been a member of a workshop group called Thin Raft whose prior existence I could have taken note of had I read more closely the acknowledgements in *The Effect of Coastal Processes*. Susan, it seemed, was the *chef d'école* for a number of the local poets.

So here I found myself, back from near two decades of exile from any community of native speakers, and surrounded by poets and poetry as I hadn't been since my fifteen-year stint in the very different context of Cambridge poetry. Reading is, in almost every way, a different kind of poetic culture. The place has never, it would seem, been in a position to put on airs. Nevertheless, its placenames and scenes can be as poetic and evocative as those from less maligned places. Take 'Cemetery Junction', for instance. No sooner had I written a poem with that title than I discovered mine was not the first to light upon it as a poetic occasion. Christopher Salvesen, now a professor emeritus at the university, had published a poem in *Among the Goths* (Mariscat Press, 1986) called 'Near-Elegy at Cemetery Junction', whose first verse reads:

Since early in the year now I've been meaning
To write a poem about this place. Cemetery
Junction: a busy spot, two main roads join
Or start; a one-way scheme runs into town –
Or (just to make the joke) through a triumphal
Arch to this tomb-rife triangle of ground.
Whichever way you look, it makes you hurry …

And no sooner had my book, *English Nettles*, appeared with my 'Cemetery Junction' in it, than Reading's own Ricky Gervais adopted the name, though the name only, for his nostalgic comedy film. If nothing else the movie of that name also serves to remind us that here, as in how many other cases, you can trust the poetry to tell the truth: for Cemetery Junction is a fork where the Wokingham and London Roads divide, with a municipal graveyard in the triangle of ground they form, and not, as in Gervais's version, a railway station.

Yet again, surprising though it may be, Reading's link with poetry goes back as far as 'Sumer Is Icumen In', the earliest English example of a round, thought to date from about 1260 and probably composed at Reading Abbey. Jane Austen's only formal schooling took place at Reading Ladies' Boarding School within the Abbey gatehouse about the year 1785. The modernist poet Basil Bunting was educated at Leighton Park, the Quaker school in Reading, but it does not figure in his mythology as a poet of the north. There are indeed a great many such moments when the town has played host, in one way or another, to writers and the literature of the nation: Alexander Pope meeting the Blount sisters at White Knight's Park in 1707, Wilfred Owen before the Great War working as a lay assistant at Dunsden and studying at the forerunner of the university, the Victorian writer Thomas Noon (Serjeant) Talfourd, born in the town and later its MP, attempting to get a copyright act through parliament over a number of years between 1837 and 1842, while in 1895 not only was Oscar Wilde notoriously sentenced to two years of hard labour at Reading Gaol, but Thomas Hardy published *Jude the Obscure*, where the town features as Aldbrickham and Old Father Time kills himself and the children of Sue and Jude 'because we are too menny'. Reading's real-life child murderer Amelia Elizabeth Dyer, hanged the following year, features in poems anthologized here by Kate Noakes and Ian House.

A number of the town's literary connections make their way into other poems, such as John Froy's about Coleridge's experiences of the town when in flight from his Cambridge student debts, or House's epigram about Lawrence of Arabia losing the manuscript of *The Seven Pillars of Wisdom* at Reading Station. In recognition of the town's long history and rich heritage, the poems gathered in this anthology celebrate Reading's connections with poetry, both past and present. Written by people who live or have lived in the area, many of them are set in Reading and the Thames valley and make reference to poems, poets, and writers that have been associated with the town over the years.

However, as is only apt for a place that is and has been a transport hub, the writers come and the writers go. Arthur Rimbaud may have spent very little time indeed here. Still, he used 165 King's Road as his contact address should anyone have wished to answer his advert for a travelling companion in southern or eastern countries. Reading is a point of intersection, where routes through the Chilterns to the north and over the downs into Hampshire to the south meet the old Bath Road on its way west. It is at the point of intersection of the Kennet and the Thames. We can read of Jerome K. Jerome's three men in their boat passing by the town, and can similarly imagine, though with no factual record I know of, that William Shakespeare himself might have come through the town to Oxford along the Thames by river transport before taking a horse to Stratford.

Unsurprisingly, many of the poets whose work is anthologized here were not born in the area, and, as they note in their introductory prose pieces, they came to the town through those varieties of accident that happen when going to university, applying for jobs, or marrying and moving with family. So this is not an anthology of born and bred Reading poets. Rather, it is an anthology of poetry written in or near, and sometimes about, the town. The place's population is in a constant state of flux, and, like London, it has seen the influx of various waves of economic migrants, as is exemplified by David Cooke's poems about his family and growing up here. If those who have resided for many years have an indelible sense of that place, those who arrive from elsewhere have the chance to see it afresh, as does the Italian writer Luigi Meneghello, for many years a professor of Italian at the university, who wrote in his memoir *La Materia di Reading* that first coming here 'was like beginning life again, with some of the vividness that we have in childhood.'

Of the many reasons for writing poetry, one is a desire to come to terms with new landscapes and scenes, to make places feel like home by a species of genial appropriation, and among the poems anthologized here there are not a few that take an unusual look at the place for purposes of both familiarization and its opposite. It is also the case, as with Elizabeth Bishop's residence in Brazil, that a stable and reassuring environment can prompt the return of distant memories. This might help explain the number of poets in this anthology who report suddenly being able to access such remote materials and past experiences in the form of outpourings of poems composed in the supportive environment of Reading's workshops, café venues, little magazines, annual anthologies, its year-round readings by visiting poets at the university or in the town, and, not least, its distinctive local Two Rivers Press.

As I say, Reading is not a place that can put on airs, and the writing it has produced in its current flowering as a centre for poetic activity is characterized by a skill basis that accords with its traditions as a place for craftsmanship and industry, whether it be for Romany caravans, biscuits, bricks, beer or books. The poems anthologized here tend to grow out of individual experience and memory, are grounded in encounters with history or recollections of people and places. There are recurrent topics which I have preferred not to edit out, such as the child murderer Mrs Dyer, the reappearance of the town's gasometers, the lion in the Forbury Gardens, and the Kennet and the Thames running through it to which practically all the poets have responded in one way or another.

Susan Utting's 'The poem that wanted to be a river', for instance, well characterizes the kinds of process by which verse finds its shape or flow – and yet I'm inclined, reading over the work contributed to this anthology, to imagine that its rivers have also wanted to become poems, that the town has been looking for writers to represent it ever since Charles Dickens declined the invitation to become Reading's MP at Westminster. I hope readers will agree with me that in *Reading Poetry: an anthology* this much-maligned town has found some of its contemporary poetic representatives.

Peter Robinson

X/10 · M 107

Adrian Blamires

The poem 'Milkwort, or Rogation Flower', written for
this anthology, is dedicated to my good friend, Adam Stout,
who lived in Reading in the 1980s and 90s. He co-founded
and edited the listings magazine, *Catalyst*, using it as a platform
for various political campaigns, most significantly against
the Cross Town Route. This scheme would have entailed
the building of a new road over Kennet Mouth, the confluence
of the Kennet and the Thames – an unlovely place for some,
with its gas towers and graffiti bridges, but for many an escape
to greenery and waterways. The lengthy battle to stop the Route
was successful, a great victory at a time when many such schemes
were being, well, railroaded through.

Kennet Mouth became a political confluence. You didn't have
to know its history to sense its importance, whether practical or
symbolic. Parties and fêtes were held there, or on Broken Brow,
just along the Thames. Badges were produced (*Mrs Coot says
'Boot the Route'*). The artist, Peter Hay, painted its 'heron-priested
shores', often from a bird's eye point of view. When he died in
2003, a candlelit boat was launched for him at a Kennet Mouth
vigil. The musician, Tim Hill, raised pandemonium beneath the
bridges, an event remembered in my own Kennet Mouth poem.
And in 1994, Adam Stout, Peter Hay and Pip Hall collaborated
on *Where Two Rivers Meet: The Story of Kennet Mouth*, the first
title under a new imprint, Two Rivers Press.

Founding the press, Peter Hay called for 'mutual collaboration
and world domination, locally.' 'Milkwort' draws upon a 1995
Two Rivers Press publication, *The Ancient Boundary of Reading*
by Adam and Peter again, with lettering by Geoff Sawers,
which maps the traditional circuit of Reading's Rogation Week
procession. Perambulators would reassert the parish bounds,
pray for protection in the forthcoming year, or simply lark about.
The map contains stories associated with places along the route,
together with musings on the wider significance of boundaries.
It stands as a kind of love poem to a much-maligned town.

I have mapped a love story on to all of this. There are, inevitably, references in the poem that some will find obscure. Clues might be found in the titles of some other works by Adam: *Creating Prehistory: Druids, Ley Hunters and Archaeologists in Pre-war Britain* (Blackwell, 2008); *The Thorn and the Waters: Miraculous Glastonbury in the Eighteenth Century* (Green and Pleasant, 2007); *Pimlico: Deep Well of Glee* (Westminster City Archive, 1997); *The Old Gloucester: Study of a Cattle Breed* (Alan Sutton, 1980). But I hope that the communal emblem of 'beating the bounds' is something readers will find attractive. Many of us take local soundings, seek out special places, whether as artists or dog-walkers, historians or fishermen. The old boundaries might be long subsumed within the wider conurbation, but some of the markers are still to be found, still to be divined.

The Pang Valley

'No pang, no poem.'

If Frost was right,
    Then what to say
About delight,
    About the way
We turn and dally
    Before this view
Along the valley
    The Pang runs through?

Flyer

Having binned the flyer from my local church,
Make Life Make Sense, on my way into town
Beside the canal, I shelter from a down-
Pour under a bridge, where pigeons perch
And gurgle, throaty and warm, on girders
Scrawled repeatedly *La ilaha il-Allah*,
A Sufi chant rising above the squalor
On nights of far cries and near-murders.

I'm about to venture out when one pigeon,
Almost white enough to be thought a dove,
Breaks from the gloom, the ammonia stench,
The dingy memoranda of terror and love,
Only to recoil from a purifying drench:
The burning unanswerable rain of religion.

Cock-crow at *The Eastgate*

Paper and pint of milk in hand,
I pass my dive of a local with its tang of the jakes
As the cockerel in the backyard defiantly takes,
At the gates of the east, one last stand.

The pub's condemned. On its sign
A figure emerges from an arch, peeling and shabby,
Leaving the faded spires of Reading Abbey
At the hour of lauds. Mumbling lines

Of faint praise, he gravitates
Through dissolute red-brick streets, darkly cowled, down
To the Thames, to stand illuminated on Broken Brow,
Awaiting the henchmen of Henry VIII.

The end of the world as we know it.
A sullied *lully lullay*, an ashen bloodshot sunrise,
The strangled notes – hung-over, lovesick, unwise –
As Chanticleer clears his throat.

In the Moslem-owned corner-shop
They know of a Day on which the celestial
Cock fails to crow. All of us, ascetic and bestial,
Falling silent (the spoon stops

Above the bowl) for we must die.
Wake up! On the front-page the Middle East's in flames,
On the *Corn Flakes* packet a bird stakes its claim:
A strangely awry triumphal cry.

Kennet Mouth

Tonight a pair of swans, heads tucked back,
Pillowed on white, float a long eddying swell
Of oblivion, black as a river of Hell.

Here, where the Kennet meets the Thames,
A river of forgetting meets a river
Of regret, Lethe meets Acheron,

An announcement I can't quite follow
Carries downstream from Reading Station –
Is this the train you're leaving on?

*

Slowly it approaches, old rolling stock,
The last train all but empty of souls,
Sparking the sky above Brunel's bridge

Beneath which, one Halloween, the Pandemonium
Marching Band (sax, tuba, accordion, drum)
Struck up a spirited dirge, struck up

A spectral replica on the other side,
Echoing to Kingdom Come in the damp arch
As torches threw shadows on the far wall.

I followed, wheeling the accordionist's bike –
The cycle path strewn with broken glass –
Past Blake's Lock and The Jolly Anglers,

The gas monitor's persistent hiss,
The lifebelt holder with its stump of rope,
The scrap of grass where we turned and kissed,

Things still in place, the things we list
To stem the haemorrhage of memories,
Words that were spoken, light on a face.

*

Issuing from the throat of the bridge,
The Kennet, brimming with volume, mouths
The same slow vow, letting go,

As it did before – the same *I do* –
Giving itself up to a greater flow
Whilst I, knowing myself undone,

Knowing it's time to go, hold back
On the brink of a cold consummation,
The clank of the train dwindling to London.

The Boy at the Well
after Seamus Heaney

It's obvious, but how many
Drawing up poetry –

The light in the boortree
A world just occurred –

Find the measure of each word
Without spilling any?

Milkwort, *or* Rogation Flower
for Adam Stout

'Madame, ye ben of all beaute shrine
As fer as cercled is the mapamounde'
Chaucer, 'To Rosemounde'

Reading *The Ancient Boundary of Reading*
From Holy Brook to Battle Mead,
From Love Lane to Cemetery Junction
   And beyond the pale,
I see the direction in which you were heading,
Leaving this town without compunction,
Emerging from that hour of need
   When maps fail.

But first they come, beating the bounds,
Skylarks, roughs and gentlefolk,
Perambulators of the zone
   That determines us,
The riverbanks and burial-mounds,
The solitary standing-stone,
The gallowstree, the *holy-oke*,
   O Terminus!

The god whose compassed steps you trace,
Following those with hazel wands
Cutting through the *brakes and bryers*,
   Ivy and vine,
Bearing the ceremonial Mace
Through mangelwurzel-fields and mires,
Following, over dykes and ponds,
   The borderline,

   To map your*self* (by accident?) …
Behind a guarded Wyvern Gate
You *lay y-bounden* in a ditch,
   In the winding ways

13

Of the Old Straight Track, ent-
ering the Season of the Witch,
Watching love disintegrate,
   A sour malaise

Infecting your Deep Well of Glee.
Time to revert, ever the swain,
Sharing roads with ancient drovers,
   Wading mud,
Free again, but melancholy,
Drawing *above all between lovers*
Demarcations, a new desmesne
   After the flood.

I mean your soulmate's sudden flight,
Your broken-winged Lady of May,
Naïf-coquette, artless-deceiver
   (This to defend her),
Recalling that Midsummer Night,
Fairy queen and homespun weaver,
The laughter as she fed you hay,
   An Ass so tender.

And so, Adam, to curious mappings,
A scholar at home with cranks and mystics
Out on the fringe, finding design
   And analogues
In tumuli and flintjack knappings,
Walking, cussedly, the line,
That bourne between the Pang and Styx,
   Pelted with frogs.

When thou yerely go'st procession
Among the ghosts you turn to face –
White Lady, Murdered Monk –
   On the other side,
There comes a calico apparition,
Gathering milkwort by the bunch
To garland hair, to take her place
   At Rogationtide.

A Female Mandrake in Fruit

I'll procure tonight through an act of stealth
From under the gallowtree, witchy, shady,
A certain flower of evil – poisonous flora
Of Eden's eastern border – to restore to you,
To *Hortus Sanitatis*, the Garden of Health,
To the Lost Gardens of Heligan and Kew,
A narcotic apple of love, dear lady,
The Song of Song's fragrant mandragora.

Here you are, figured, the one I seek:
A rosette of sinuated ovate leaves,
Head of globular orange-red fruit,
The intertwining limbs, filamentous weave
Of a bifurcated life-giving root,
Her pulled-up little catch-breath shriek.

Jane Draycott

I live on the border between Berkshire and Oxfordshire, in a
street that in five minutes takes me to the banks of the Thames
in one direction and the chalk woods of the Chilterns in the
other. For years, my sense of my home landscape was formed
from the ancient views that opened up on our weekend walks
on the high paths and bridleways: flint, chalk and beech woods
that rolled away and down towards the hidden river. Then in
2001 I spent six months as poet-in-residence at Henley's River
& Rowing Museum and the view changed.

Like coming down to Google Street View level, from down
on the water everything looked richly different. I spent three
winter months out on the tugs and barges of the Thames
recording the working watermen and women, and when the
weather improved I attempted to learn how to scull on the
wide stretch of the river near home. Now I saw the hills I had
walked on in a reverse dynamic: it wasn't that the hills swept
away down to the river, it was that the valley arced out from
the water as a rib-cage flies out from a spine. Once out on
the Thames, I saw that rather than dividing the two landscapes
of its opposite shores, the river unifies them like the body
between two wings, in the relation so memorably held in
Peter Hay's iconic Two Rivers heron logo.

The imaginative river is treacherous with over-used imagery
and tropes, and the Thames especially seems already full
to maximum with its provision of literary dramatizations:
the dark river of Dickens and Conrad, the nostalgic river of
Grahame's *The Wind in the Willows*, the dreamy, hallucinatory
river on which Lewis Carroll composed his extempore stories
for Alice. I have only one poem on the wall by my desk,
a Thames poem – 'Canoe' by Keith Douglas, which seems
to do everything that can be done, in sixteen lines that Anne
Stevenson has called 'perfect'. Like the unmentioned railway
tracks at the heart of Edward Thomas' 'Adlestrop' (once,
of course, part of Reading's great GWR hub), the river lies

at the heart of Douglas' poem – the 'somnolent river' which knows it is 'allowed to last for ever', the central core from which the landscape of the south of England radiates away and elsewhere into history.

Prospect

'Some believe that new developments will allow us to rise
above our nature and live for hundreds of years'
Peter Healey, *Tomorrow's People*, 2010

Anyone who wanted to could leave, could gather
    shivering on the south side of the river,
labelled and provided for with socks and sweaters
    and a little cash. We walked across the water
in our thousands and left behind for ever
    all that was great: the monuments and sewers,
cathedrals, theatres, mothers, lovers, brothers
    as the flames licked at the city's raging heart.

Faced with the prospect of living forever,
    we headed for the country lanes together,
imagining the *parties de campagne* among the clover
    and the stories each would tell the others
on the way. We had left behind for ever
    all that we had loved. It was a start.

In Memory of Henry West

who lost his life in a whirlwind at the Great Western
Railway Station, Reading, March 1840, aged 24 years

Not expecting the future in so soon, he turned
and looked for the swarm of bees. Down the lines
that had never met and never would now, it came,

the hum of the barely discernible: ribbons of flies
in a sheep down a culvert, the crack of the ice-plate
under a boot, himself in the fog.

The iron work announced his name, then the flat
hand of the storm pushed him towards the gap.
In the eye of the wind he saw himself, halted forever

in the freezing cattle-wagon of the third class waiting room,
stopped on the table top of a Siberian winter, surrounded
by bears and the icy stares of commuters, and round him

further and further, the dopplers of a thousand 125s,
the high speed sleeper and all the other sleepers going west.

from Uses for the Thames

'"Feather !" cried the Sheep …'
Lewis Carroll, *Through the Looking-Glass*

The test was to dip
the needles into the dark
of the swallowing mirror

and by pulling to row
the weight of your own small self
through the silvery jam of its surface

trailing behind in your passing
your very own tale, knitted
extempore from light

and then to lift them,
feathered, ready for flight.

The Hired Boat

They wanted a boat that would ferry them upstream
away from the chaos of sea, a boat
named *Shalott* or *Narcissus* which rowed like a dream
while they took it in turns to tell stories or spoke
in brief fragments that surfaced then sank in the mud.

They rowed into darkness, its wingspan or rib-cage
of hills, up the glassy spine of the valley,
each stroke like a heartbeat or turn of a page.
By morning they'd vanished, their boat in the shallows
no more than a leaf or the eye of a bird

which drank at the glittering throat of the flood
where it narrowed to only a single word.

The Road

Travellers leaving their horse overnight at the prehistoric Ridgway site
of Wayland's Smithy believed they would find it newly shod by morning.

Full once of the kind of folk you might well hope
to meet, this field or street's deserted, empty
even of footprints. Of the ancient shoe by the side
of the road, of the articles dropped and of the suitcases
no sign or symbol at all. More than the question of oaks
or beeches, their age or purpose, is the wordless army
of fence posts, the deliberate mist which gathers at night,
frost's covert displacing of stones from the rock-face.

And now here's this turn in the weather: the storms
which arrive like a shipwreck from nowhere, the consequent wait
in a lifeboat, tipped like a cup to the lip of the tide,
the stowaways eyeing their feet, spectral and blue with
the distance they've travelled, shoeless and hopeful, from home.
All the locals are able to say is that promises made
have yet to be kept, that firing starts around midnight
and travellers passing will sometimes make offerings or music.

Up at the House

So sorry if I have offended you
by that poem up at the big house
sorry eaten at the edges is discovered
behind the gun cabinet, a small intense thing
requiring all their powers of detection.

I just put down the first thing that come
to me beyond the formal garden
a birch wood of nervy pathways is seen
striking out across the field line,
thin limbs fired by an unexpected sun.

If it isn't the poem that has upset you,
what has that poem which is
so hungry, that cabinet so curious about
what's locked away and who is who,
the power of fire and motives gone astray.

You glare at me as if I'd committed
a murder. Please burn this together
with all records of whatever's happening.
On no account leave it to smoulder
or hold it near to your body or ear,
the most dangerous thing in the house.

The italicised text is from a note found during work
at The Vyne (National Trust)

Wayzgoose

Waist-high the wheat is talking, the great
conversation. We motor past, foreheads
to the glass, and climb through hedgerow
margins to the edge of the known world.

On the hill's broad back, offered like snow
without a sound, we now lay out
the argument and patterning of our feast.

Where we have come, summer applies
its even weight to tarmac, cornfields
and the silent lake where no ink lies.

Where we are going, the goose has
in her eye and takes her onward flight,
nib-neck leading toward the season
of quiet work by candlelight.

*Wayzgoose: annual excursion for printing employees,
traditionally August 24th (St. Bartholomew's Eve)*

Peter Robinson

My experience of Reading before moving to the town in the spring of 2007, after almost two decades living in Japan, had been restricted to the descent from the Chilterns into Caversham, round the concrete-sided relief road, and on to the Hampshire coast, where my first wife's parents lived. Those fleeting encounters left me with a sense of the landscape round Nettlebed and of rural Hampshire, interrupted by a ghastly bit of planning-blight that had cut the town in two. Yet visiting Reading first to be interviewed and then for house hunting, I discovered the sort of post-industrial, semi-rural town I'd known in my northern industrial childhood. The sense of such a displaced recognition first came to me, and most forcefully, on the Kennet canal-side, coming face to face with what remained of Huntley & Palmers. It was as if the old factory had baked a Proustian biscuit taking me back to a moment in childhood walking with my family beside a tannery in Liverpool. Reading, it was clear, would be a home from home.

A poem called 'Huntley & Palmers' about that moment of confused recognition, the first I completed here, was collected in *English Nettles* along with other poems that built up my first responses to settling in Reading. The selection anthologized below adds others from a slightly later moment, when the initial surprise of living in the place had begun to wear off, but some of the realities of daily life and work back in England had started to sink in. All of these are set either in Reading or in its relative vicinity. Even the longer one, 'A Little Exercise', set in Christchurch meadows, Oxford, was completed from an earlier draft because we had come to live in the Thames valley and could make day trips up river. Reading is still surrounded by fine countryside with a large number of stately homes open to the public, and there we would take the children to introduce them to the scenery and history of one of their parents' native lands.

My poems almost always begin in specifically located moments of encounter, and the detailed circumstances of these occasions provide embedded metaphors for the significances that I sense need to emerge in the processes of composition. So 'Graveyard Life' is set among the memorial stonework at Cemetery Junction, whose entrance arch had already inspired a poem of that name included in *English Nettles*. Into these patches, other glimpses of landscape and of bereavement insinuate themselves. 'The Returning Sky' similarly began in changes taking place in our immediate environment – autumn coming, trees being cut down, and surface rainwater failing to drain away. These years living in Reading have already prompted me to write quite a large amount of new poetry doubtless stirred by finally returning to the kinds of sky under which I spent my first thirty-six years.

Huntley & Palmers

1

Then that tightening in the chest
and tear-duct, like a taste
of whatever it might be,
comes with the looked-at brick façade
seen on a canal bank walk
but in so much perspective,
with the strollers' voices
heard as if by alien ears
(ones too full of other views,
views, reverses and reversals)
as if from somewhere else.

2

That taste could be digestive biscuit.
A sudden scent of wood smoke
rises across locked, sluggish water
where a drowned white bicycle
seems to float up from the depths.
Further, assailed by all this flooding
laburnum, ivy, rape field yellow,
wisteria that thrives in the good spring
weather, there's a memory of pain,
of pain, though not of its sensation –
no, no, I wouldn't be without it,
looking at what's left, and gone.

Graffiti Service

The aerosol boys have been at it again
making signature loops and swirls,
soccer boasts, names of girls
on stone, glass, concrete, pebble-dash house-front …
You said I should take them, citing me,
as welcomes: we'd gone past a substation door
decked out in swathes of graffiti.
So I daub the town with words once more.
But, today, council workers are out on their round
depersonalizing public space
with industrial spray-gun, solvent and paint –
like an artist preparing a ground.

The Bird-Ghost

Like winter breath on a pane of glass
sprayed with fixing medium,
like a burglar's greasy handprint
or white ectoplasm trace,
that bird of prey had hammered hard
against the built environment.

You could pick out its bent beak's blunted face
and from a slow-motion film,
the flicker of that wing feather stain.
A smudged bird, arrested in headlong attack,
its output of energy equal to its impact
on the unseen or unforeseen
(our bedroom window pane),
it had made such a stunning mark.

A Little Exercise

'All in the golden afternoon
Full leisurely we glide …'
Alice in Wonderland

'They hadn't gone much farther before
the blade of one of the oars got fast in
the water and *wouldn't* come out …'
Through the Looking Glass

Down, down in the river meadows,
beyond a long oak drive
with its contested histories
that they'll have witnessed and the towpath's
interrupted shadows,
we take our time about it; we arrive
where boathouses are set back from the brink,
activities get under way,
the scullers bearing shells above their heads
will float themselves out on the current,
and it makes you think …

This early on the river, now, an oarsman
backs into his morning while
a bike-rider with megaphone
is bellowing words, words of advice
at the viewless stylist
who makes you think he's anyone
effortfully distancing a past
of dowdy summers, overblown
ambitions, yes, as we glide on
by weeping willows with their ghosts
of *sfumatura* leaves.

Out of a sticky, shade-mottled day
here come its dark towers

silhouetted against late afternoon sky;
and the day, as done by Seurat,
sees me moving like a fish back in water.
Later, through grass voices rise.
They're language students' macaronics
unmixed before, recalling
consonant clusters from remote skies
and, haunted by them, I catch snatches
of a future in quotation.

That squirrel's gnawing at a pizza,
holding it in small front paws
and coaches call out jargon to their scullers,
figures pause on famous bridges
hearing jazz or chatter borne
by pleasure steamers, flat-iron cruisers …
You can't pull and give advice at the one time;
to left or right our two girls guide me
backing, with uncertainty,
on a zigzag course towards
futures made of words.

Across the landscapes with dead dons
I'm looking out for further clues,
for traces of what happens
when everywhere's soured by quarrels, civil wars.
Conflicted signs of histories
have turned from us, give little away.
Silence fills the avenues.
Then it's like they're oblivious,
have had enough of crowds like ours
gone into deepening shadows
under the dumb oak trees.

Graveyard Life

'there are no countries in the world less known
by the British than these selfsame British Islands'
George Borrow

for Tom Phillips

Glimpses of the Muntjac deer
in cemetery undergrowth
are rubbed out by what place-names hint,
where signposts point
around its arch of quiet life
with cedar, willow, privet, yew …

The cemetery, needless to say, a dead-end,
its far brick wall
backs on terrace house-backs,
the devil in all their detail –
a cat shooed off an outhouse roof,
cascading frozen ivy …

But who would have guessed that here,
where criminals were interred
beyond town limits and a crossroads gibbet,
idling one afternoon
I'd meet a safari photographer
with barrel lens and tripod
in search of the sacred or scared?

Who would have guessed that Muntjac deer
surviving by carved angels
(like creatures off old land mass edges)
would point to one more great unknown
under my nose, in this hemisphere?

Credit Flow

Rescued from a lost afternoon –
I wasn't much company for anyone; but
you drove me out of that aloofness,
not far, to where farm chimneys
shared a sky with flustered trees.

By the flooded gravel pits,
seeing migrant species fly
suddenly in their fancy thousands,
it's as if I needed the assurance
of wigeon, teal, mute swans …

or reassurance of a day,
a wintry dusk like any other
and its chilly wind
threatening one more snow event –
another day been lent to us,
but not to be returned.

Wood Notes

Shadows extend on pine-needle beds,
across the undergrowth ferns –
as if long life's decrepitudes
had stalked us through the woods.

A beech tree trunk bore scars of old loves.
You saw sun patches in the high leaves
and felt birch-bark striations.

It was like standing by a family tree
to get back with your sense of touch
things mislaid down the years.

I remembered Linnaean classifications,
woodnotes you were straining to hear
or words both our parents said
and caught us unawares …

The coppice paths were seed-strewn then.
A bird's nest on an upper bough
drew eyes from family, still unforgiven;
but none of that mattered now.

Reading Gaol

'the salesman … knows nothing of what he is selling
save that he is charging a great deal too much for it.'
Oscar Wilde, 'House Decoration'

Reading gaol from Reading town
(*Homebase*, to be precise)
has weed-tufts sprouted from a chimney pot,
one crenellated central tower
with apertures barred, still rising above
sheer, featureless, brutist walls.

There's a sunset blazed across glass façade
where we go to cost soft furnishings,
to match non-toxic paints.

From a customer car-park, Reading gaol
imposes high above the flow
of rush-hour traffic round a roundabout;
so that's where he would learn the price
of everything there was to pay …

Receipts checked in a bloodstained dusk,
the glint of its lit windows
and perimeter arc-lights about the new wing,
by Reading gaol, I see
where if you killed the thing you love
you'd die in earnest, that's no jest;
where, his social credit spent,
they would kill the thing they hate
with the power of the State
and, really, a trial cannot end like a play.

Gasometers

'Le souvenir vivace et latent d'un été
Déjà mort, déjà loin de moi …'
Raymond Roussel, *La Vue*

Seen again from the First Great Western,
'This town's growing on me,' said
the passenger, slowed towards its station,
where two routes converge.

Thick gas pipes snake from underground
to cross the Kennet's course
beside a red-brick rail bridge,
water reflections speckling its arch.

*

Now the old tank's all but empty,
its structure open to a sky
flecked about with bits of cloud,
a man's head in the framework spaces.

'Politician,' you guessed out loud,
photographed to make his point
above the biscuit factory houses
or boarded up pub windows …

*

I liked them too, could see better days
in an avenue's baking roof-tiles,
a loaded pear bough's greens on brick,
grey structures up above the trees;

and all my future hopes, ambition,
to be read in black & white
like an end wall's painted advert
faded, years back, by the sun.

*

To think of them, gasometers,
depressed, lost like that advert
uniquely able to appear,
when light falls from an angle;

of bifurcated time at last
entwined by their faint reek
into a parallel belle époque
materializing from staled air,

*

sharp-cut shadows, splayed leaves
blued, reflective of this sky;
and they call back possibilities,
the summer, say, of '75 –

its fugitive touch come to the rescue
in an airy jump-cut series
emerging from the crowd to kiss you,
still here, still alive.

The Returning Sky

Blocked, the drain-flood lake out front
is like a dirty moat now.
Workmen come sucking-up sodden, black leaf-fall;
the surface water seeps away
and there we are, before this house,
with a fresh access of sky.

The neighbour fir trees, opposite,
succumbed to saws in daylight
and that's what gives us so much blue
to populate with relatives,
acquaintances or others' loved ones,
last things, the latest cry …

This season too has done its bit;
gone, our deciduous screens.
Bare branch-shadows on a white house wall
make more intricate vein-work,
and they're added to the flooded gutters'
leaves painted-up with sky.

Now our lately dead are in the air.
An overcast grey-scale dusk's
shot through with thin red cloud streaks;
and, look, they're everywhere
in privet hedges, like a private grief
for the targeted to die.

You incorporate them, part and whole –
synapse, nerve-end, heart brimful,
as any body knows:
it's like death were a white van driver
who had splashed us differently,
indifferently going by.

Kate Noakes

Writing about place is part of identity. Whether we like it or not, where we live is part of who we are. I came here as an undergraduate in 1980 and, although I have travelled widely and even lived in different parts of the world, I have made my home in Reading for the last thirty years, and Caversham for twenty-five of those. The locale features often in my writing, as setting or as the source of a narrative that might have a wider or even polemical meaning. If I'm lucky, I might discover a poem behind a report in the *Evening Post*, or I might literally find a poem on the street: 'RUPERT AND HILARY / (found on a Post Box) / If anyone knows this couple / about to marry, / a card was left for them / in St. Peter's Avenue.'

I've spent many hours fossicking in the museum and been rewarded with three of the poems here: 'Women's Chronicles', 'Aelfgiva in Tehran', and 'Silchester Autumn'. 'Women's Chronicles' gives women, for the most part the silent witnesses of history, voices and the chance to speak about their lives. It is deliberately feminist in that regard. The reproduction of the Bayeux Tapestry is a rich vein for poem-stories. Again I was drawn to the women – there are only three of them. The parallel between the depiction of Aelfgiva and the treatment of women in contemporary Iran resonated with me, hence the poem. Finally the ghost of a Roman woman walks though 'Silchester Autumn'.

Crossing it at least twice a day, the river Thames is central to my daily life and it seeps into my poetry. The Thames and the Kennet are such important geographical features of our town that they can't be ignored. Two poems here celebrate the mystery and threat of rivers. 'Evaporation as Prayer' was written in response to the residency at the Turbine House on the Kennet (Blake's Lock Museum) of artists Ann Rapstoff and Hilary Kneale in the summer of 2010. Ann and Hilary invited Lesley Saunders and me to give a river-themed poetry reading as part of their work. The poem distils my response to their art and the environment; true ekphrasis. There is some wonderful countryside around Reading, especially just north of Caversham on the edge of the Chilterns.

Walking there often leads me to think of our environment. In these poems I explore green choices in 'The Question' and 'Rape' and food miles in 'Unknown Variety'.

Women's Chronicles
Voices from objects in Reading Museum

Bess Crookshanks – The Oracle workhouse – 1628
Oracle workhouse doors

Lanolin softens my rough hands.
Practised and quick, I thrill
in my new trade. On a morning
I produce near one hundred rolls
for my neighbour to spin.

Food fills my belly,
the children have warm feet
and Squire Kendrick
approves our manufactures.

Alice Clark – St Giles' parish – 1640
Church chandelier finial

I cannot recall, this forty years past,
the number of screaming brats
I have ushered in, slapped and tucked,
the Besses and Williams, nor those
unnamed that shunned this world,
nor yet the feeble mothers.

I have prospered, my good service
valued in hard coin. This day
I extend my beneficence
upon St Giles' and am invited
to choose bible or bauble.

Thirza Challis – Minster Street – 1796
Lead deed box

My companion is silent now, her feathers
wrapped in silk and lead where my good deeds lie.

Two grave days have passed since
her Yuletide song gladdened our hearts.

Mine is heavy as I place her under the floorboards
to perplex thieves and future generations.

Mrs Dyer – baby farmer – 1896
Facsimile of poster reporting a murder trial

I did it. He told me.
Out of their misery.
Unwanted by me,
despite the pay.

I slipped them,
quietly in turn,
unlucky little Moses,
all six of them into the river
at the lock.

Dark, cold.

They went silently.
I hear their crying no more.

Aelfgyva in Tehran

*Aelfgyva, the mysterious lady, is one of the three Saxon women
in the Bayeux tapestry. She is pictured being struck on the head
in a panel the precise meaning of which is apparently unclear.*

Before the quick stone pins my temple
with its final prick, know
that I am basely charged,
sans witness, sans cause.

You've brought these men to point at me,
call me bitch, tricked them along
with promises of what,
honour, virgins?

They are false and strange to me.

I've been quiet here this while
embroidering pashminas,
cloistered indoors
with a pattern of flowers.

There's no mystery. I'm no naked witch.

As you flick back
your woad-coloured cloak to give it
freedom, motion,
I catch your practice:
the strike and kick.

Won't you finish this in public,
somewhere open like the market?

Silchester Autumn

Thin days, and a shade heavies her heart.
She makes a line by walking the damp grass,
mourns the slow rotting of unpicked plenty.

Her dew Latin rings for months
as hips are frozen,
defrost and freeze again before falling.

Her foot stubs a pot lid, Samian ware.
She remembers Gaul, its ruddy sun,
grape harvest, the last time she felt warm.

She goes with the bite of winter at her heels.
Chill air nips her throat. She checks
the fruit knife tucked in her belt,

its silver and mother of pearl handle is glowing.

Rape

Prairie-fields in Bank Holiday rain
seed my eyes
with their yellow pain.

Evaporation as Prayer
for the Turbine House Artists' residency, June 2010

This is where clouds form indoors
from the holy water of Knock,

the snow that fell on my garden,
rain from an electrical storm.

If I had the keen eyes of a heron,
I might see droplets spinning

in the diamond air of this house,
each fresh circle of hydrogen,

oxygen, hydrogen, each miniature mirror
of the world turned topsy.

The room is full of Ganges, Nile, Thames;
if I could choose, it's a good place

to drown, though these black stones
are too large for my pockets,

so I'll wash them on the tarred boards,
and keep them out of the river today.

I'll dream of lotus and cabbage weed
another night, swim only in the tin bath

and imagine the source of drip-rings
is a ticklish trout intent on a deep pool,

waiting for my leaky body.

The Question

By the M40 southbound
to Uxbridge, a sign
along the side of a field;

a simple question
painted one letter
on each fence panel –

why do I do this every day?

and everyday several thousand
commuters smile,
and carry on their way.

Unknown Variety

For days an apple tree on the A4,
that might be Laxton's Fortune or James Grieve,
sinks its branches under a weight of fruit.
This year's mighty harvest turns from blush
to crimson richness.

No-one comes for such a ripening,
though in passing many point
to the roadside on fire –
lighting the dullest of dull commutes.

There's no safe place to stop and gather,
no pull in on the road from Maidenhead
and the canteen has cartons of sweet juice,
foreign apples, bushels and bushels.

Colpo di Fulmine, *or* Love at First Sight

When you can least predict it lightning breaks
from its cloud-bonds, forks the sand,
makes something rarer than meteorite:

silica glass, fulgurite, yellow as diamond,
yellow as Chihuly, yellow as gold,
fused in the chaos of the desert.

This palm piece, the size of a phoenix egg,
is a comforting weight with its round
coolness and facets that fill my heart.

But I must remember its flaws: a longing
for lamp-work, for green-houses,
for windows on the sides of sky-scrapers.

It might shatter and me with it, so I wrap it
with care, lock it away 'til dry days
when its memory can't be tricked

by the damp or sudden charges in the air,
lock it away if summer fills with buckets,
lock it away from the static on fire-fly night.

John Froy

These poems have a theme of birds in Reading, often in the redbrick semi-industrial townscape around the Kennet and Newtown with its landmark gasholders; there's a brush with the Royal Berkshire Hospital, and reference to a couple of writers' encounters with the town. I like to use place names as keys and anchors: 'Battle', Brunel Bridge, Goring Gap, the IDR. A few years ago there was a swan's nest on Crane's Wharf, an amazing sight this great heap of sticks and feathers with a sitting bird beside the towpath – probably too close, for they didn't return next year. Or was the messy nest and guano cleared away?

It's getting much smarter around the Kennet now, but a walk along the towpath to the Thames is still a visit to Reading's past with its old warehouses and wharfs, plus the odd supermarket trolley in the canal. I was surprised too, to see a line from *Macbeth* as neat graffiti ('Looking for Kingfishers') – cultured taggers here. Graffiti appears in another poem, about Lydford Road near where I live. It's cleaned off, reappears. There are citizens who keep a look out, scrub it off themselves, or report it to the council. You think they (we) are winning, but then fresh rashes appear on the cleaned walls.

This brings to mind those two writers with Reading connections: Oscar Wilde, synonymous with the prison, with whom I linked a red kite that was wheeling above the Homebase roundabout one day ('For Oscar'), and, a century earlier, Coleridge ('S.T.C.'). On the run from his creditors, the poet enlisted in the Dragoons and was stationed at the Bear Inn in Bridge Street (a medieval hostelry demolished in 1910) under the alias Silas Tomkin Comberbache, a name he'd seen on a shop front–how Reading!

Red kites were re-introduced to the Chilterns in the nineties, they're suddenly everywhere. We can all see these gawky raptors flapping and gliding around the town, in an odd throwback to Tudor times when they were a common scavenger. Are they cleaning up our roadkill? Goldfinches are back too. Caged and cruelly treated for centuries–written about and painted since ancient Greece – they visit feeders in suburban gardens freely now; they trill gorgeously from the holly tree next door ('Charms of Goldfinches'). And those swans turn up again in a squiggle of spilled paint from my brush as I paint a window in a quiet Reading street.

Mute Swan

On Crane's Wharf, another development:
mound of sticks and feathers by the gravelled path,
sitting bird that hisses and shifts –
it's the last piece of ground left.
So what is a family of swans worth?

Looking for Kingfishers

It's sleeting down the Kennet.
From Duke Street to the Brunel Bridge

stolen trolleys, raced, hoiked,
lie upended in the steely water.

Along the towpath threadbare buddleias
hang offstage, roots gripped to cracks in bricks.

Sprayed (with care) on a freshly-painted wall:
FAIR IS FOUL AND FOUL IS FAIR –

an omen for all this riverside housing:
water levels can go up as well as down.

Will the swans nest on the wharf again?
Will smart-clad coots build on rusty iron?

By the gasholder at the far end
beauty glides past in a hat and scarf.

Fresh Graffiti

Down Lydford Road: tortoises, bollards,
a convent and a primary school,
STUNDENTS OUT scrawled on the wall.

Back-street cut between the blocks
where children swarm, joggers dodge;
scoop bins fixed to posts don't work.

When it goes quiet a resident
patrols for litter, fresh graffiti,
reports her findings to the squad.

And here's a new urban scheme
of scaffolding and beige paint
inviting more street art.

Don't know about this or Mr Whippy
parked outside the school
belting out Klaxon tune and fumes.

And no one knows who's dumped
the blue velour three-piece suite
the students shift around at night.

For Oscar

Above the roundabout's curve,
along sheer prison walls,
I watch the easy flap and glide,
the hover, cheeky dip and rise,
show-off of a rust-red fork
from the new bird in town.

S.T.C.

Silas Tomkyn Comberbache
(taken from a shop front),
on the run from his Cambridge embarrassments,
joined the 15th Light Dragoons.

He lost the six-guinea bounty
to a pickpocket straightaway,
marched into Reading dinnerless
on Christmas Day.

Hopeless on horseback, saddle-sore,
erupting with boils,
he mucked out the stables,
rarely remembered to polish his sword.

But in his billet at the old Bear Inn
comrades recalled the love letters
Samuel Taylor Coleridge
had helped them write.

His brother got him out:
'Insane, 10 April 1794, fee 25 guineas.'
The rust of a sabre lies somewhere
under the Oracle or IDR.

Nurse Tracy

Brian's been doing his Breathing since six,
John greets everyone who passes his bed,
Tony is safely back in the armchair
after a night in the corridor with nurses;
he's on the phone telling 'Jill' all about it.
It's morning on Battle ward.
Peter, still nil by mouth,
waves at the tea trolley that won't stop.
And Nurse Tracy's back on shift.
Pale, scrubbed, her hair tied up,
she's bringing round the medicine trolley,
hands out golden apples.

Charm of Goldfinches

Here they come on a backend afternoon,
trilling through the gardens, our patch of urban sky,
a large family living round here now,
new townies perched on the ridge tiles and wires:
Goldies, Redcaps, King Harrys, Petaldicks,
linked with Hera, in Pliny, in Bosch,
in the Fabritius painting we found online,
in Clare and Hardy, chained and caged.
Still singing, they swoop from holly to feeder,
their stand-in for thistle, teazle and burdock,
acrobats painted with seven colour splashes –
the real wonder, they are still here at all.
We watch in close up from the back room
and then they're away at some hawk alarm.

December Birthday

The gasholder rises at the end of the road,
there are still a few leaves blowing around
as I set off for London.

Mum would be eighty-one today –
I can't post her a card from the gallery
as I set off for London.

Her own birthday was always too much,
it drove her into a spending frenzy;
Christmas for us came to mean anarchy.

While under the bed lay her old portfolio,
untouched: parent portraits, family pets,
lightning sketches in cafés, waiting rooms.

I'll look for Gwen John cats on darkened paper,
linger in the Tate shop as she would have done
on the train for London.

Red Kite

'When the kite builds, look to lesser linen.'
The Winter's Tale

Red kite! Red kite! The puttock's back.
Tudor street cleaner we almost wiped out
has spread across the Chilterns; Goring Gap
to Maidenhead, returned to the Thames towns.

See the rusty fork-tail, rakish wings
swoop on a roadkill, perform
an aerial circus in the park,
harry hang-gliders in long loose flight.

Now urban gardens watch your backs,
the hat bird and clothes-line thief is out.
They build their nest of sticks and leaves,
adorn it with knickers and polystyrene.

She sits, he keeps watch, in the edge-of-town beech;
all that sparring and clasping was bonding for life.
On ragged summer wings they teach young to fly,
Oxford Road to Woodley, and over the motorway.

Painting Windows

The brush bucks and flips in my hand:
this unwatched moment, something
expressed or unexpressed that creates
an arabesque, a dance of paint
clear across the shadowed pain;
Pollock splatter, Zen drip, Rorscharch blot;
swan's neck, flying crane.
                              Shift on the ladder,
wipe the glass clean with a turpsy rag.
It might be art but it's in the wrong place
and it won't earn my living. Again
bring the brush to bear on the thin white line.
the tight white line where glass meets wood,
and the water seal is made – beautiful.

Claire Dyer

Many of my poems are about relationships; with people and with places. I am particularly interested in both the notion of home and the symbiotic relationship between looking forward from the blade-edge choices which shape our futures and looking back at the echoes those decisions leave behind. These themes therefore inform the poems in this sequence.

I met my husband in Birmingham, where I was working at the time and had just bought my first house. A year later we married and moved back to Reading. As I had grown up here, getting married was also therefore about coming home.

'Nine' uses the August 2010 meteor shower as a motif to compare ideas of domesticity with the 'unknowability' of space. The wishes in the poem are ironic of course!

'The Red Kite and I' and 'Designing a Bowl' deal with change and pausing; the process of reassessment which is natural when one's children grow up. Again, I centre these emotions on images of domesticity and the idea of predestination. 'The Red Kite and I' was written in honour of the stunning creatures which fly above our house in Earley. I sometimes feel it is they who actually live here, and that we are mere visitors; their kaleidoscopic eyes seem to miss nothing.

'Umbrella, Broad Street' explores the awareness of self and heritage in a cityscape, and 'Humming' continues this theme of change, concentrating on travel, both virtual and emotional. I often think of Reading as at the axis of a crossroads; after all when asked why we stay here, my husband and I often say it's because it's so easy to travel away from. As such I fear that we don't appreciate it enough for itself, so the last three poems are placed firmly in Reading.

In 'Crescent Road' I investigate Reading's marvellous multi-culturalism and contrast it to my much more prosaic, suburban childhood; the idea of the doll crying 'real' tears is designed to throw into relief the actual suffering of children in the Third World.

'At Blake's Lock' expresses the fear that in amongst the bustle, commuting and head-down-everydayness of life, there is the chance that we can forget where we come from, who we are, and whose lives we have touched and been touched by.

Nine

In our August back garden,
hands high to the reach
of Perseid's tail, the cats' eyes
looked yellow envelopes up at us,
wondering why we were
unusually there, and we counted
nine of them – shooting stars,
landing amongst the rips of slender clouds
and treetops, and behind next door,
and we made our wishes, nine of them,
each one colder than absolute zero,
no bigger than a grain of sand,
and then we went inside to wait
for them to come true.

The Red Kite and I

are both hunting in the high heat; the difference
is he's powered by history and wind, by ripples
in the sky and the colour blue; he can feather-flex,
hover, pivot, bend; his eye can see blade-thin shifts
in the grass, be magnet, filing, king. I am not
these things; am hunger-heavy and soil-stuck,
am pauper, water, waste; am grounded
by every fable ever told, by the bitter-wish of want.

Designing a Bowl
Caversham Arts Trail, 2009

The house is small, dark, temperate, restrained,
only its corners catch the slantings of sun.

Heat presses its windows with the force of hands
and she envies it its secret corridoring,

its storybook of angles, front to back, which
remember her first home, where she lived alone

before she chose the stretching of bricks,
the flattening of grasses under her children's feet.

The garden here drips with the privacy of flowers
as she touches the glaze, smoothes the imprint of text,

looks from drawing to ceramicist and hears
the whisperings of another life.

Umbrella, Broad Street

She opens it like scissors to cut the rain,
its points are sharp and slicey and her grandmother's
warning's a hum in her head not to run
with it open to the pull of the wind.

It's city-street black,
or shoe-shopping pink,
has buttons and catches and a sheath for protection,
and over her head the rain falls in fragments.

Humming

Last night in my pillow
Great Western trains
pulsed journeys to Wales,
car doors closed, stars
fizzed winter above
pylon and streetlamp,
vixen barked trembling,
teeth white in the moon,
and towards dawn the first
plane from Heathrow rose
to a crystal of birdsong,
soft breath of the cat
coiled at my feet, pluck-tug
of a sleepless guitar
in the room next to mine,
blood-beat in my ear
and the half-held humming
of dreams, the trying-to-remember
of a voice I'd once known.

Crescent Road

I passed her inside the tender arc
of Crescent Road; to my left a trim
of Victorian houses, their parlour-stepping
ghosts, to my right the flat-pack Community hall
where my babies were weighed
and measured in the long-ago
of cradles and happy-ever-after songs.

The sun was low and warm, bricks blood-red,
leaves rustled conversations in shy
collective voices as I bounced the camber
in my hot blue car. She looked on with wide
assessing eyes and stepped a graceful
road-side dance in wild-print orange chiffon,
fruit in a *Happy Shopper* bag Temple-balanced on her head.

She made me think of home, a sturdy house –
the type a child would draw – with curtains
at the windows and a bright red door.
I'm inside, in woollens, with my OBE grandpa,
the one who bought me toys; with *Cluedo*
and egg-mayonnaise, and the special pink doll
that could squeeze 'real' tears from its clear plastic eyes.

At Blake's Lock

I had forgotten the river,
its sound and its waterfall,
the green of it;

forgotten the launching
of birds, the heron's
plastic watchfulness,

its only movement an eye,
a feather-flick; forgotten the reach
of trees, their branch-dipping

offerings and tang
of pillow-soft leaves;
forgotten the sun's marbling,

its mirror-darts of quiet,
secret dreams; forgotten
the scoop of oars,

glide and scull of boats;
how we closed our eyes,
white-blinded by the sky,

but could still see; how time
rested on a blade edge,
unblemished, cloud-light.

At Blake's Lock I remembered
these weir-real things,
and the rush of them, and you.

Gill Learner

In 1966 my husband's company relocated and I moved, with great reluctance, from London. When I told an acquaintance where we were going, she said: 'But people don't *live* there, they go through it on the train!' I had indeed passed through it at least three times but on foot from Aldermaston to London on CND marches. For the first year or two I found Reading slow and dull but gradually it became 'my town' and now I would hate to move back to 'The Smoke.'

When I retired from teaching Printing and Media Studies at Berkshire School of Art & Design, it was with the intention of returning to writing, which I'd abandoned thirty years earlier on my return to full-time paid employment. I'd had a few successes with short fiction when I spotted a competition in the *Independent* for a limerick on the subject of time. I entered and, to my astonishment, won. The prizes were lavish – a two-week holistic holiday on Skyros, flights and transfer included, and, more significantly, membership of the Poetry Society. 'But I'm not a poet,' I bleated to the competition organizer on the phone. Indeed, I hadn't written any poetry since somewhat Gothic efforts in my teens and had read little although I very much enjoyed Ruth Padel's 'Sunday poem' in the newspaper. But in no time I was hooked on the genre – both as reader and, very soon, writer. My first published poem appeared within a year in *Poetry News* and I felt I'd really arrived.

Since falling into poetry, I haven't written much specifically about the town or its rivers, primarily because, with the Thames at least, so much has been written already. The chief exception is 'Belonging' which was runner-up in a competition organised by the River Thames Society and was published in their journal and in the subsequent anthology *The River Thames in Verse*. The subject was initially my husband's grandfather, whom I had known, but he evolved into a fictional character.

However, the river has had quite an influence on my writing. Workshops run by Jane Draycott at the River and Rowing Museum, Henley, and the associated exhibitions there, have produced several poems including 'A Sense of the River',

'A Single Scull Takes Flight', 'River Rising' and 'From Grilse to Kelt'. 'Rain, Steam, Speed' has a Thames connection in that the painting is of a scene near Maidenhead Bridge.

Among the topics I find most inspiring are technologies, particularly printing. Family and music are other sources of ideas. These are reflected in my choices too.

Belonging

Best forget the dream: a gilded day with sugared grass,
breath fluffed round our heads; a crystal glide
from underground to scatter light before we clouded it
with Grandad's dust. The infant stream had sprawled,
hidden its birth in lakes which once were fields.
The river writes the rules.

At least the wind was with us, pushing its breath
along the flow. It wafted floury particles but let grit drop
like winnowed grain from the parapet of Ha'penny Bridge.
For a second, ashes scummed the swell that
simmered east then clotted, swirled, went down
as the river received its own.

He was a Millwall man, whose living Devlin did for,
last in a line of stevedores and lightermen
with muscles like mooring ropes, hands of seasoned teak,
who'd seen water stained with indigo, coal, blood;
and women who'd scrubbed shirts which smelled of lemons,
cinnamon, tea, tobacco, or sewage after a fall:
the river's not always cruel.

Let those crumbs carry in the drift to where brine begins
then sink and settle, add to silt on stones he skimmed,
fragments of letter-freighting bottles, pins that fastened
matchwood rafts he saw propeller-churned to splinters.
From eighty years ago when the moon governed these games,
the river ran through his dreams.

He turned a bitter back as cranes swung over building sites
and the rattle of anchor chains gave way to shouted deals
from would-be Whittingtons. As houses grew
    where cows once grazed
so that Kennet, Colne and Wey were forced downstream,
and winter water spilled and spread back across ancient plains,
he shook his head: *Will they never learn?*
The river always wins.

From Grilse to Kelt

The undark of the ward snuffles round my bed.
I lie weightless, exhausted but taut
with elation, adrift on anglers' lore:

how a fierce tide prickles in the gathered fat,
urges the salmon from rich feeding towards
one-way water; how she aims her snub

at the bland flow which tries to redirect
the motor-force pushing her on. Skin tarnishing,
she dodges night nets, growling knives, circles

below a weir to find the deepest scoop,
builds speed for the muscle-clench projection.
She rises with the temperature, reversing the run

of fork-tailed fingerling to find the gravel nest
she struggled from. Into a new hollow
her wasted body gives up its amber beads.

Emptied, we slide together in the slow descent;
let the downstream carry us towards the sea.

A Sense of the River

Here is a congregation of empty fingers,
gathered together over years: blue
as the Piccadilly line, vivid as Arsenal strip,
creamy as St Paul's. These didn't

snug the hands of surgeons or beauticians
but their touch could be as delicate – tickling
the hulls of refuse barges, disco boats;
soothing pier supports and steps. They stroked

the limbs of washed-up Barbie dolls,
fumbled in burger boxes, frisked oyster shells
for pearls. They arpeggio'd on bike wheels,
jingled the xylophone of roof-tiles jostling

on a beach, castannetted broken plates.
Pock-marked by chemicals, blistered by oil,
they survived the pricks and tourniquets
of hook and line. But without the puppetry

of tides or hands kept safe while hefting
breeze-blocks, laying tarmac, trimming joists,
they're lifeless, subverted into art. Now
there's only thumbs up or a V-sign at the past.

*Michael O'Reilly collected objects from beside the Thames
and grouped them by type for an exhibition of photographs:
'Fragments from the foreshore'*

A Single Scull Takes Flight

Early mist ghosts the trees as I ease
inside the turquoise shell, balance
on the river's skin, find a beat: extend & flex,
extend & flex, with breath to match.
Life's in suspense – cattle still confused
with sleep, no smoke from narrow-boats.
The river bears me up, nurses me along.

In dreams I rise, weightless:
shell segmented, riggers
turned to gauze. I catch moths,
mayflies; hover, reverse.
Hell's mare, ear cutter,
devil's darning needle
threading water, reeds, air.

The downstream's warmed my blood.
I turn against the flow, fill my lungs
with morning, gather power to fight
resistance in the muscle of the flood.
Now trees are more distinct; the wake
is highlighted. A blur of sun's
just visible – round and medal-bright.

Rain, Steam, Speed
by J. M. W. Turner

Look how, against a weight of strange beliefs,
the hare lopes from beam to beam
between the singing bars then hears above
a harrow's scrape and dancers' calls,
the growl of some strange creature larger
than a horse, deadlier than the blades that shred
his field in shrinking rings; hears the growl
become a roar and, scalloping the air,
stretches to escape the iron and smoke,
westward through dissolving sun and storm.

Poor hare, that in this new millennium
cannot outrun the train.

River Rising

This water has no meniscus, will not
be bounded, will breach our certainty.

We watch the inching through gravel,
the spill over door-sills, bubble

of carpets, darkening of oak.
We back from it stair by stair.

Banged Out

Some days his right hand forgets its cunning. Although
it knows the case like Ellie's body, suddenly it muddles
p and *q*, fails to lock up tight, ends with pie.

Between times he could weep at newspapers with titling
not kerned or letterspaced, *f* and *i* unligatured, flyers
home-composed in a mishmash of typefaces.

Some days his feet forget the way. He fumbles
his key into a long-ago lock, snarls at the new owner,
at Ellie arriving to steer him home.

Usually, though, he changes his shoes as soon as
he gets in, asks how she's been, washes up without
a chip, remembers the grandchildren's names.

Today, even after several in the pub, he walks straight
and tall through the crash of chases and galleys,
the cheers of comps who didn't serve

their seven years, wouldn't know an em quad
from a quoin, depend on algorithms to split words.
He's the last of the hot metal men.

But today is a fine day.

How To Build a Cathedral
in memory of Ralph Beyer

First sweep the ruins for unexploded bombs;
sift rubble for what to keep; clear blocks dressed
centuries ago. Now lay roughcast stone on stone
into undercroft, chapels, porch and saw-tooth nave.

Leave gaps. Fill them with angels scratched
on panes or allelujahs of many-coloured glass.
As furnishings: a cross of timbers black with fire;
Christ in glory on a floor-to-vaulting tapestry.

Find a man, a refugee, with skill and flair. Give him
words and tablets set into the zig-zag walls.
In a nave unholy with welders, masons, scaffolders,
watch him sketch, breath curling, on the stone.

Eccentric capitals grow from the chisel's bite,
line on line. He brushes off the dust, tilts his head
to judge the fall of light. No two letters are alike
but amassed they sing. They sing.

Don't ask his faith or how his mother died
or whether in this place of reconciliation
work is freeing him. Admire the craft, how it
blends into the whole – this covenant.

Counted Out
In memory of Grandad Harold 1884–1972

It was quite a jump from Highbury to Amiens,
from hefting sides of pork to stacking the cart
with crates of bully beef, barbed wire,
steadying the nag when thunder
crumped too near, crooning what came easy
to an ostler's son but couldn't always
still the flinch of hide; and no good to grow
too fond of a handy screen.
                          It was a far cry
from feathers, Maud's rump in his lap
and Little Connie's dreams a reach away,
to a doss-down in a blackened barn,
the shift of hooves in the splintered night,
trying to block out yells by reliving bouts
at Clifton Star A.C., struggling to recall
the brine-smell as they trundled in the chara
to Southend.
                It was a long, long way, chlorine
fizzing in his lungs – caught before he'd time
to tie a piss-soaked handkerchief over his face –
to the scurry of nurses, soothe of milk,
and the cough that never frightened off
the ten a day of Craven A until
it all went quiet.

Quartet for the End of Time
by Olivier Messiaen

It seemed that the horsemen
had broken through the seals.

Men scuffed between huts:
snow creaked under clogs
that gnawed their feet;
breath blurred heads,
settled on patched uniforms
wrenched from defeated troops.

When the aurora borealis flushed the Silesian sky,
one Frenchman's faith hardened.
Because there never was enough
black bread or cabbage boiled to rags,
his dreams rang bright as cathedral windows.
He pinned eternity to a stave,
shaped hope in sharps and semiquavers;
shared his vision.
Cracked lips called birdsong from a clarinet;
swollen hands flicked at piano keys
to conjure gongs and trumpets;
fingers barely thawed
stopped strings
as two bows spun prismatic arcs.

Four hundred men
barbed-wired together
fattened on rainbow music.

Ian House

In a recent survey Reading came second in a league table
of Britain's clone towns, where independents have been squeezed
out of the centres by chain stores. It confirms Reading's reputation
as the place you have to pass through to get to London or Oxford
or the West Country. So why stay here? Inertia is one answer.
But perhaps there are others.

When you've lived in a town a long time, it's a palimpsest.
John Kendrick's seventeenth century workhouse-factory at the
Oracle, which crumbled into tumbledown sheds, has given way
to a consumers' paradise. Dickens often stayed at the George;
Coleridge, on the run from his creditors, hid here as a dragoon;
Mary Russell Mitford's house is a thriving dental practice;
to walk along Valpy Street is to remember a man known to several
generations of Reading School boys, and with good reason, as
Dr Wackerback. So '*Faux Pas*', based on the Forbury lion, links
the Afghan wars of the nineteenth century with today's campaign
while 'Shells' remembers the passing of one of the three Bs (beer,
biscuits, bulbs) on which the town's prosperity was built and
'Mother' goes behind a closed door in the most banal of streets
to peer at a startling evil.

Like towns the lives of individuals are multi-layered. 'Snow
Man' reflects on what happened to the son of a Spitalfields fruit
merchant, a Jew, who rose from being a cabin boy at sixteen
to the height of the legal and political Establishments.

'Celebrity' thinks about the relationship between a man and
his legend and yet 'Natural History' celebrates the intense joy
there may be at moments in the most humdrum of lives.

Then again, every step is fringed with personal memories:
a street corner that marked a parting of ways; shops where
presents were bought; houses inhabited by vanished friends;
a glimpse of an extraordinarily beautiful woman. I walk through
collocations of experience that may become poems. 'How We Are'
remembers one chance meeting that was itself a palimpsest.

By contrast I spent the whole of 1998 working in Moscow and
two poems here, both fairly recent, look back on experiences
in that weird and wonderful city which Reading throws into relief.

And there are always the rivers to lead you out of Reading and out of yourself by winding along the towpaths to Goring or Newbury or who knows where and by looking down into the inscrutable. For rigid, land-locked humanity, water is a profound and necessary experience of the other: of what is fluid, shifting, gentle, irresistible. 'Masterstroke' and 'Awash' touch on some of the relationships between men and rivers.

William Penn, who addressed the Quakers here when they met behind what is now RISC and the Global Café, said, 'This is truly a town of meeting: of the waters of rivers, and of these Friends in a place kept tidy for the spirit ...'

Natural History

There was also an Andean condor with a leathery head
and a neck stiff and red as a penis, a peacock
trailing bracken and butterflies, a pebbled guinea-fowl,
a snazzy lorikeet and the long, yellow claws of a falcon
sweetly curled round a bar while, outside, hundreds
of people were walking from one place to another

but I cannot stop thinking
of a lead coffin
the size of a jewel box
found under the floorboards
of a house in Minster Street
containing 'T. Challis's bird.
Died December 27 1796'

and of how T. Challis wiggled his toes at dawn,
quarrelled, smelt the brewery on the wind,
of how a finch flared its yellow-black wings.

Celebrity

Changing trains at Reading in 1919,
T. E. Lawrence lost most of the MS
of *The Seven Pillars of Wisdom*.
Probably a sneak thief. But what I see
is a stack of paper, neat as an officer's uniform,
swirling in the wind like a robe.

Shells

'The air spoke' to Midge Harris, alone
in the bared factory, listening
('holding the room to my ear'),
to Muriel's jokes about pricks,
to the girls bashing tins

while dough glimmered, cement-heavy,
was paddled and pressed,
and glissaded like coins over rollers
to the glare and blast of coal ovens,
to women's swift, mechanical fingers
packing bourbons, garibaldis, osbornes
and arrowroots brittle as love lives

and Albert Woolley, fifty-four years
in the mixing-room (three making cartridges)
emerges, soft and white,
blinking, sticky with almond paste.

Smiling Captain Mason
was photographed at Gallipoli,
resting a polished boot
on a wooden crate
black-stencilled 'H&P Biscuits',
'Handle With Care'.

Faux Pas

Thirty-one feet from the nose to the tip
of its whiplash tail, sixteen tar-black tons
of muscled flank and rocky mane,

the Maiwand Lion, pedestalled, striding
over the dahlias, slumbering Goths
and ladies in frocks in the Forbury Gardens.

'It's wrong-footed,' we told one another for years,
'for all of its cast-iron, imperial confidence,
an anatomical impossibility. No wonder

the sculptor killed himself.' We weren't the first
to have got it all wrong. All but eleven
of the 66th Berkshires were killed

(outside a garden, as it happens)
because 'a handful of rebellious tribesmen'
were 40,000 Afghan soldiers armed with guns.

In the bronze parade ground of the dead
each name flares to shirt-sleeved life,
then stiffens to a ram rod. A plane

snails in and out of clouds. At St James's
a wedding party is a froth of lace and smiles.
I watch the plane release its clutch of bombs.

Pigeons shit on the lion's head. Its century-long
resentment growls along the gravel paths.
There are no goldfish in the pond.

Mother

Amelia Elizabeth Dyer, baby farmer. Murdered at least thirty babies.
Last address: 45 Kensington Road, Reading. Hanged 1896.

Nothing much to see, a house like any other
in this terrace between workhouse and board school:
brick, two-up, two-down. I hurried past
the fresh white door, the glittering windows,
yet smelt rotting meat in the kitchen and climbed
to a room in which someone must dream
of Mrs Dyer's slug-flesh face, soft eyelids,
smooth hands, long and tapering fingers.

Neighbours hardly knew they were puzzled
when babies entered that conjuror's box
and vanished. Mrs Dyer loved poetry,
found a thing to do, wound the edging tape
three times her little throat around
and jerked it. She let them die quickly.

It's more than a mile to the Thames.
My feet beat out the names:
Doris Marmon, Harry Simmons, Helena Fry.
The parcel grows heavier. She called herself Mother.

How We Are

It feels like the scuffle of a key
at what might be the wrong lock,
then slides home and I find,
in a cradle of plump cheeks,
her face at eighteen, a Meissen,
her rueful eyes (ah, yes, blue-grey!)
and, as my lips press soft, remembered flesh
(her ribs were warm beneath their skim of silk),
we're caught in an uprush,
a sparkle and spatter of waves
till our eyes flitter for clues, for scars
and we're left high and dry
to semaphore gauchely.

'Lovely to see you': the requiem chime.
She's replaced every cell in her body
but, as we turn to the rest of our lives
and she sways down the street,
she's dancing through a joss stick room
and I know, looking back, that I knew,
without knowing, that the girl
was the woman she had to become.

Snow Man

There is a marble Viceroy in the Memorial Garden,
high-collared and thin-lipped, swagged with medals,
mantled in ice. The right hand is hooked
round an imaginary lapel. His hollow eyes
survey the destinies of millions, his titles and offices.
I search his face for the shivering ship's boy.

*Rufus Isaacs, Marquess of Reading, 1860–1935: QC, MP, Solicitor-
General, Attorney-General, Lord Chief Justice, Viceroy of India,
Foreign Secretary. George V Memorial Garden, Eldon Square*

Somewhere in Moscow

She picks up a carrot and slices
the feathery green from the frost-blackened root.
There are hundreds to get through
and you know the street, brown with snow, crawls
for a mile and three-quarters, that they drop
in the pail like the minutes
and days of this featureless woman
wearing two rusty coats tied with string
and you want their rough skin in her hands
to bring back the marl round the dacha,
her mother's lace collar, the wink of a match
in the bowl of her grandfather's pipe,
the birch forests smaller than hope.

Slow Fade

Not, now, even an album: churches
salmon, turquoise and gold
cooling to monochrome.

A woman floating a tablecloth,
spreading it near the steps to the Metro,
laying out knives, forks, three towels,
a smart red skirt, a small glass cat,
a yellow lampshade and a carriage clock.
(Or was it somewhere else I saw the clock?)
Sadness rises from lino,
absence waits in a drawer.

Standing outside Kiev Station,
fifteen women in line,
behind a gauze of falling snow,
heads bound in layered woollen scarfs,
a bottle of vodka in each mittened hand:
they seem to board the dark green trains,
like grannies in a Giles cartoon,
and dwindle for a thousand miles to 1943.

What's left is always
a jigsaw of pottery,
a fretted iron spoon.

Masterstroke

Your feet follow the dips and bends
of the towpath or the lie of the grass,
rushes are bent into huts and hairdos,
catkins flirt in the breeze,

a coot snails upstream
on a diagonal, half-drifting,
half fighting the current
so its bill misses nothing,

the wind teases a flickering
network of light from the water
to a boat's white bow:
a galaxy forming and fading.

The oarsman, headed wherever,
inscribing the watery steppe,
looks for eddies and snags,
for advantages. The river submits

to muscle and will, to the robotic pull
of the blades, the swift scissors
till on the bend, as he feathers,
stilled, poised in his shell,

he's the keystone that locks into one
clouds, willows, water-birds, river.

Awash

Today willows are growing in mid-Thames.
It could be Flatford Mill: always about to rain.

Constable loved 'slimy posts, & brickwork',
knew how water gets everywhere,
rots barge-boards, softens a mortar course,
turns leaves to Shippams paste;
knew the comfort in decay,
the ease of flaking, drifting off.
Even the canvas, you'd swear,
is damp, wetness a condition of being.
His fields cling to your boots.

Here too the earth's gone soft. Willows
have the look of a new species. The Thames
slobbers at the bank or sprawls, generous
and terrifying. Against its tonnage,
yielding, inexorable, one swan
battles, butting through rubber.

Once a companion that ambled alongside,
its surface quilted or gunmetal smooth,
molten glass over rocks, it's a travolator now
the colour of vomit, speeding Coke bottles,
fag packets, an old tyre, a spinning coot
down to London, out to sea

while we slosh, hilarious,
through these bewildered fields,
our eyes renewed, bodies happily colliding
as fooled gulls screech across the sky.

Wendy Klein

I grew up in a family of passionate anglophiles where the River Thames, with its strange silent 'h' and short 'a', entered my vocabulary and my imagination early; first with Kenneth Grahame, later with Charles Dickens. I never once dreamed I would live in England myself. Had I done so, it might have been the something-to-look-forward-to that got me through my childhood and adolescence in bleak inland California towns. Once here, I never got over the excitement of the river despite living in Pangbourne, a five-minute walk away from the Thames Towpath, for twenty years. To stand on Whitchurch Bridge on a summer day and watch the boats pass under it in either direction: towards Reading, towards Oxford, was to be delighted anew each time. Better yet, to stride into the face of a chilly wind on an autumn day when the summer people in their hired boats were gone, the water ruffled and brown, the trees nearly bare, the river returned to us, the locals, its true 'owners.'

Turn the corner and the Thames sidles past, was the opening line of an early sonnet I wrote about the river when I first began writing poetry in 1998. The sense of privilege in turning that corner, catching the first glimpse of the river and the meadow, never left me, though I might do it more than once in any given day, my spaniels tugging at their leads, eager to hurl themselves into the water to play fetch. Swimming dogs, swimming children, and we did swim in it, too, despite dire warnings about leaks from AWRE Aldermaston, suspected links with childhood leukaemia. Indeed, our first spaniel loved swimming so much, that when she died we brought her ashes to the water's edge and scattered them near the jetty where she would launch herself repeatedly, returning sodden and exhausted, only to demand that we throw her Frisbee again.

A community of dog walkers frequented the river, strolling or running. Lively conversations developed between locals who only knew the names of one another's dogs. Dogs attracted the interest of the boat tourists, who often brought their own, and if the dogs made friends the people made friends for the day or the week. There were boats that returned again and again each year – narrow boats, quaintly painted, with flower pots brimming with trailing geraniums and bicycles strapped to their sides for shopping trips into the village. A small hippy commune travelled in each summer on a battered old boat with its name, *Another Seagull*, painted on it. The more staid locals all worried the owners might be selling cannabis to the village children, but no one ever actually caught a whiff, and their children were wondrously beautiful with their long tangled hair, printed cotton frocks and bare feet. Mooring was strictly limited to a week, and the River Warden, an old woman, clown-faced with make-up, her skin raddled with cigarette smoking and whisky, patrolled regularly, shouting at people who had over-stayed.

Dependable Light

Museum, Reading Town Hall

I want to stay in this room where young girls
once came to learn art; its blues and whites Dutch-
clean. Here the floor is etched with knots and swirls
and wood-worm tracks – feels warm under my feet. I want
to have arrived in my huge rain-proof cape, its hem heavy
with street-mud, to have shaken out my skirt that just clears
the floor, kicked off my boots, peeled down to leg-of-mutton
sleeves. My smock will be drizzled with yesterday's spatterings,
and I'll scrape my hair back into a serious knot. In a turpentine
trance I'll fill my lungs with risk, but keep safe as tiles in the tin-
glaze of windmills, of tulips, to blacken my fingers with charcoal;
mark out the form of the day's model; her angles and slopes;
the sheen of naked flesh rubbed white by my thumb, where tall
windows offer up dependable light for work on this leaden day.

Orienteering for a Blind Dog
for Simcha

In place of a map, there's the tip
of your nose pressed into the cradle
of my thumb and forefinger.

For your compass, the rustle
of my boots in long grass, the crunch
of pine cones, the tap of my heels

on hard ground, our secret whistle
that tells you when to stop, when to go,
and my voice that warns of a low wall,

or a gap in the fence too small for you to
pass through. Pheasants too clumsy to fly,
the neighbour's cat, are reduced to distant

memory, a passing scent that makes you
raise your head, lift a paw to give chase.
How I'd love to remind you

of the splash and surprise of a river swim,
the mystery of rubber balls that float, the
wild hunt for a Frisbee

in an un-mown field, when you check
the wind for the time of day, turn for
home, ready for food, the high point

of your life. *Give a dog your heart to tear
apart*, said Kipling, and he knew, so I'm
left with the puzzle of your docile

acceptance of what I with two-legs and
a much bigger brain, find so deeply
unacceptable; the proof

of that tired old adage – *what the eye
doesn't see* – the way the heart's
not meant to grieve over it.

Sunset through a train window on the 16.48 from Paddington to Oxford, January 2008

Every shade of red is displayed out there –
the sky a Louisiana crawfish boil,
and I glance at the woman next to me – dare
her to put aside her slick magazine
while I fail to stop myself from gawping
at this battlefield – fire engine, tangerine.

The red gene sits on the x chromosome,
so women see more shades of red than men,
and yes, she's looking now burgundy's come:
sangria, persimmon, Persian, burnt sienna.

Borne from some faint Darwinian reason,
this shared red-sight has fitted us better
for making fires, staunching blood, gathering
berries, mining rubies, sunset-watching.

And Another Thing

My neighbour says we've had fly-tippers –
at the top of our field; our field
where I walk my dog each day,
but only round its edges,
because it's usually cultivated:
wheat last year, feed corn the year before.

I go up there to have a look, and sure enough
there's an old fridge, already starting to rust,
some manky kitchen cupboards,
raggedy edges and peeling paint,
drooping in the weeds
alongside planks of garden fence,
the wood rotting, the weave loosening.
My dog sniffs at a decaying deer's head
slung over the fence by a hunter or a poacher

while I stand gawping at this country lane mess
that mimics graffiti in the town;
think how daubing old railway carriages,
the sides of flyovers,
even the occasional building,
makes more sense somehow; the temptation,
or even the invitation, of the empty wall –
the way that Banksy turns it into art,

but this rubbish has no logic –
our hospitable field,
its tangle of wildflowers in spring,
rabbit warrens, summer crops,
that we can't protect with barbed wire,
electrical current, the law, or even love.

News of Spring

Dandelion clocks are telling bad time;
wild mustard so high it swallows the dogs,

til shivering blossoms give them away
as rustling, they reappear.

Siberian ducks shake crested heads,
in just-thawed-out surprise,

while mallards, less exotic, glisten nearby
as we watch the riverbank

erupt into spring – try to keep pace. I use a buttercup
to tease out your fat secret,

but sullen as water you avoid my invitation,
turn away, brush off bright petals, frown.

Chestnut candles flare as an aeroplane ploughs
a furrow in the sky. Queen Anne's lace,

you note, resembles the trim on christening bonnets,
and babies were never agreed.

Flood Lines

Under chiaroscuro clouds,
swollen with yesterday's monsoon,
I stumble out lead-footed
in scarlet wellingtons, and cautious,

paddle through the new-born swamp
where river and meadow meet:
a vast mud puddle,
that bewilders the wildlife.

A small brown rabbit bolts at my approach,
and two cygnets, escorted by an angry parent –
riding shotgun – ineffectual against
nylon fishing lines. Under my mac

the skin prickles with damp, though no rain
falls from the sketchpad sky; smudged
and well rubbed in, it settles over the meadow,
over my spirits, in suffocating grey folds,

where the artist's thumbprint is obscured
or non-existent. The wind is skittish with autumn,
but I'm pleased to see how it teases the water;
pleased to have made the effort to see.

Plenty

Take this field of feed corn, a buffet laid out
for red deer, muntjacs, or a banquet
for vagrant squirrels.

Pheasants sashay down its aisles; guinea fowl,
their silver heads bobbing, weave in and out
between stalks that are Oklahoma high.

Only to our knees on moving day, we've watched it
in all its in-betweens – waist high when the books
were unpacked; just past our shoulders

when the paintings were hung – now towering
so far above our heads it shuts out the road,
the horizon, the hills spattered

with rusty gold. We stand in an aftermath of empty cobs
rashly harvested by the creatures who share
this place, who warn of paucity ahead –

lean winter, uncertain spring. We gather dead wood
for our first fire keep an uneasy eye on
the nettles, the fuel gauge, the headlines.

Downstream

Well, I'm swapping waterways again –
not so far this time as the first – from the sea
to my Connecticut at dusk – its inlets,
its mysteries, the implacable frame houses
perched on either bank, their eyes intent
on our last night together, my first canoe.

So much greener than the next –
my San Joaquin, the exact shade of valley mud,
the slap of water skis that summer before uni,
skinny dipping, the secret glow of first sex
before the flight home.

Then across the sea to the next one: the Loire,
Orleans, Chateaux Roux, before the icy plunge
across borders to the Isar, the Frauen Kirche,
sombre the year round, her onion domes
reflected in ripples season after season–

five years not to fall in love with its prim banks,
its too-orderly flow, as opposed to my brush
with the Mississippi, brief, if rich and disturbing –
like holiday romance – too dangerous
to hang around for long, and finally

to where the Thames laps domestically
against narrow boats, offers its quiet surface
to children, to dogs, encourages picnics despite
the constant threat of rain. In the end
it's the synchronicity tantalises – all rivers,
one river, the roads in between lives.

Muntjac

Not your everyday pet, he says, the young
stable-hand, shakes mud and grass from riding
boots, with you draped over his arm, dangling
stiff-legged, all points pointed: hooves, dainty
but sharp, needle nose softened by your doe-
still gaze, braced for tears. It's the gaze disturbs,
shapes what comes next; how can we venture out?
The waiting room is hushed with our shared guilt.
Each of us will drive tonight through dark lanes
where creatures may blunder into our paths.

We invite him to jump the queue; the deer
goes first, a tacit pact. As the door shuts
we breathe out; speak of journeys that may end
in small deaths, and he comes back empty-armed.

Paul Bavister

Many of these poems are about times of transition. Creeping floods, decaying buildings and storms create landscapes where people struggle and survive. In the face of slow disasters relationships change, sometimes leading to compromise but often generating honesty. Thoughts of a simpler life go from dream to near disaster.

These themes were developed during attempts to live outside of what I saw as a destructive culture and which led to long sessions on Bulmershe allotments. I first visited the site in late autumn and was confused about the boundaries of my plot. After kicking through the long grass I found raised paths where stones had been piled and a number painted on a sheet of iron. The spade I'd brought bounced off the hard grey soil and would not part the grass roots. A few days later I returned with a fork and managed four or five rows, shaking out the roots and piling them to the side of the plot. As the weeks passed and a wet winter created slippery clay my mind started to fill with the site's loneliness, enhanced by the constant roar of the road beyond the fence. I thought more about what life might be like in the future. That future was without oil, electricity, complex technology. On the shortest day I dug a trench. The sun was a deep orange and hardly made it above the trees. I could look straight at it through the mist. A kestrel waited for me to disturb rodents, dropped down into the long grass. As I completed the trench it slowly filled with water. I was tired, slipped and slid down into it. Lying on my back, freezing water soaking into my jacket, I felt part of a dangerous, threatening environment.

I climbed from that strange grave and within days my writing started to change. I pieced together neighbours' ideas about the area, how names connected back to a flooded land, crossed by cattle, bears, sea eagles. An osprey was sighted crashing onto a local lake. I felt the flux in the landscape. As the soil warmed other allotment holders appeared and I found out more about the history of the area and realized many of the crops I'd hoped to grow were out of the question. The bull's marsh had never been built on due to its ability to turn from field to freezing pool even during weeks of dry weather. It also seemed that the cutting for the new road had drained some plots nearest to it but left those close to the woods sinking deeper. My plot sat somewhere in the middle.

Many of the poems in this selection come from this sense of past, present and possible futures. The allotment flourished in its first year, pretty much failed in its second, then with the application of tons of muck grew again. The possibilities started to seem more positive. I'd grown to like week after week of beetroots, marrows, potatoes and beans. The subjects for my writing had become set in mud.

Earley

The eagle's scaly feet crashed into still water
dragged up a thrashing carp. That bird
was a baby stealer and we wanted it dead.
We wanted to know what it tasted like
fill ourselves with every fish it had snatched
from beyond our rods – stitch its feathers
on our sodden coats set a candle in its skull
but wading into the icy lake was risky
and anyway we didn't have a rope to climb
to its nest or an axe to chop down the tree
and even as we cursed it crashed
onto the lake and dragged up a carp
that would feed us for weeks.

Jackdaw

A spiny chick, slate grey in white ash
struggles from the fireplace to your cupped hands.
The chimney rustles with another nest.
We both know I should have netted the pot –
your sigh says I've been mollycoddled,
I'm soft, washed out, washed up.
You wrap the chick in a cloth.
I bring a pinch of cat food from the fridge.

By autumn I'll forget to knock out the nest.
Then you'll stamp from the smoke filled room
point at the chimney and curse me.
This year's jackdaw will have joined
the others swirling up on your rising heat
then dropping at your feet to be fed.
You will curse every chick you've turned
into tatty, stinking, useless birds.

The Mechanic

My jacket has flown away with the moths.
The car drips oily rust – mechanics never
ring back. I've moved too far out – this place
was cheap for a reason – grubs tunnel walls,
soften the log pile, blacken bags of flour.
Beetles burst from filthy sacks with my
winter's warmth and food in their guts.

Weeks later I hear a car on the track –
a mechanic who never rang back,
who fixes my car and gives a glance
that makes me glad I live alone.
He leaves a spanner under the seat
and later it swings out on a deadly bend
and gets stuck under the brake. I'm alright.

I take it back to him past the scrap yard
to the garage block. Axels and wishbones
drip their blood. The beak of his welding
mask reflects sparks rising from the carcass
of a car. I place the spanner on the tray.
He nods and I know that very soon
I'll be seeing him again.

Wolves

Should wolves be released in the country park
between the airport and the reservoir?
I chased the question through focus groups
sifted complaints from fearful dogwalkers.
Local papers on the library's microfiche
showed a bestiary of old horrors
a teddy bear's picnic of swollen managers
cutting tape with the mayor –
a project to release a young eagle
that within weeks snatched
a terrier by its tartan jacket
and used the meat to fuel
its long flight back to the Swedish cliffs.
I met a ranger at the reservoir's edge
who made me feel like an idiot –
he was like the prince of a forgotten island kingdom
focussed on the wolves' release
retreating to his hut on stilts but leaving me with
the wolves will be tagged and tracked by satellite.

We Laugh Without You

I'm up and down the wooded slope
bundling sticks, dragging logs
piling them against the freezing house.

Black pebbles slip from the flooded bank
grit pours from the tree root steps.
The muddy path slips past parsnips, beets.

It's a time you would have called the salad days.
Not pre-packed, washed but scorching cress
alive with bugs in soggy bread.

You might have dug us free from this mud
stopped theorizing about what we'd lost
worked harder, faster than the food we ate

given us time to sit for an hour and let
our wrinkled skin dry out. Or you might
have sat by the fire and eaten up

every spare mouthful, kept us working
into the soggy night. All I know is
that without you we often fall silent,

every slice of the spade goes slower,
we're not sure what is planted when,
when we laugh we laugh without you.

Cormorants

We watched cormorants on the radio mast
angle oily wings to the watery sun.
They dropped, followed their beaks

in straight lines to the sea.
We scoured beaches for plastic bottles,
ropes, anything useful.

The cormorants have measured our nights
slapping flat feet on steel struts.
Once I drifted off and dreamt of their bodies

streaming with silver bubbles, of them
diving from black rocks where storms break,
their long bodies filling with fish.

When I woke I sat up, looked back
at the thin fold in the blanket
where you'd passed out from hunger.

Later that night a sudden silence woke me.
I got up and found you standing at the window
watching the mast and the cormorants

angling their spiny wings at the moon.
On the sill you'd unpicked a nylon rope
made a fishing line, a plastic spinner, hook.

Ghosts

These mushrooms will give you
a never-again hangover, missed
heart beats and suspicious lumps
under your arms. But *these*
feed you when you're fearful
of another meatless, beanless meal,
when your hair starts to blow
away in the winter wind.
So we search where the last
bark chips have spilled across
muddy grass, we peep up
from the carpark's edge then
run to the spinney of thin
birch trees. It's here that
you'll find the givers and takers
both opening their sticky caps,
wrinkled stinkers pushing up
from buried beams, burnt boards.

Acacia

The acacia thrived
for three hot summers –
bright yellow pollen
between grey green spines –
the local bees
struggling it back
to overheated hives.
Then summer black clouds
tipped freezing rain
stripped the tree
to shiny white –
cracked branches creaked
with cormorants and gulls.
We went from fussing
over flowers and shrubs
to raising beds of sodden soil
with planks split
from the garage blocks.
That spring self sufficiency
went from dream
to reality, kept us hungry
for months until the gulls
took over the wrecked flats –
we scrambled up
with a nylon rope
filled our bags
with warm eggs and chicks.

Victoria Pugh

I came to Reading to do my teachers' training in 1974. I hated it. To me Reading was: Cemetery Junction, The Jack of Both Sides, chain stores, takeaways, the echoey, empty tiled entrance to Reading University in London Road. I was lonely and miserable, stuck in digs in Whitley, doing my teaching practice in a large comprehensive. A year later, leaving, I promised myself that if there was one place on Earth that I would never live again, it was Reading.

But fate had other plans in store for me. In 1988 I returned with my husband to the South East. We did our best to find somewhere other than Reading to live. We looked in Wallingford, Goring, Henley, Watlington – everywhere! Eventually we decided we could only afford to live in Reading and moved to Caversham.

And you know what? I'm really glad we did. I've lived in Reading for twenty-two years and I've been happy here with my family. I've made many friends and met diverse, interesting and unusual people. I found the strength, the teaching and the support to do the one thing I'd always wanted to do – become a writer.

Reading and the surrounding areas appear in several of my poems. I am interested in what lies beneath the surface of things. On the face of it, Reading is like many British towns: full of traffic, jobs, shops, money, deprivation, entertainment, green space, grime, crime. Beneath that, there is another layer of Reading. If you look hard enough, if you scratch the surface, you can see it. For example, on the way to Primark on West Street, look at the W I Palmer Memorial Hall, with its mock Norman archway and you'll find it is decorated with little faces – cherubs or green men with plants coming from their faces. Much is hidden in Reading; it's there for anyone to find. You must love Reading, with all its faults, and then it will open up for you.

If you walk down a street every day, or often enough, you notice its changes, its wintering and weathering, and the decoration and care lavished on buildings by previous generations. There is a sense that the town is shifting and moving, within its own time frame – though we, trapped in our own time limits, may not always sense this. And, of course, though sometimes I see things in Reading that make me sad, I often see things that make me laugh.

The countryside around Reading is its counterpoint. It is beautiful and varied: the tight-budded thorn that arches over Ridgeway paths; the 'wide grin of the countryside' that meets you as you come over the brow of the hill as you drive out from Reading on the Woodcote Road; the tree we found in Crowsley Park; the river, the beech woods, the downs.

So that's Reading for me. It's shifting, it's fragile and it's stuffed full. But somewhere beneath all that, there is its layered core. You look hard enough and you'll find it.

Shelter

Women walked past me
and boys kicked me after dark.
Seedy men offered me
a fiver, at a price.

I picked up my things
and walked through the town,
towards the wide grin
of the countryside.

I found the hollow tree
I played in when I was young –
crawled in with my bags,
and made myself at home.

And it's warm in here,
living in the oak's heart,
with the occasional oozing
of whatever sap that's left.

I climb up and sit in the branches,
and the oak and I
become a wooden Buddha,
with birds resting on our shoulders.

Love God

The man with the backpack of green things
walks down the path that crosses the earth.
He throws clover and grass on the track,
it grows up lush and sucks at his shoes
as he pushes them through the grass's spit.

He strokes the silver ripple on the wheat,
bends and enters the arch of white thorn
as the flowers endlessly tighten their grip;
throws stars from his pack, and they stick
in the branches and make heaven for us.

He sprinkles bitter fields from his bag
some Wild Garlic or Old Man's Beard,
burnt earth and stubble, many are fallow.
Then he's gone, somewhere, down the road.
He's emptied his backpack of green things.

St Anne's Well, Caversham

She checks for water, where there's none.
Today, a woman's looking up at her.
She stares down through an iron grid
at a bore that's cut into layers of years.

She waves, the woman waves back.
She is trapped below her watery bars.
All the light she sees is a round of sky,
at night, only the glow of streetlamps.

She walks along by Reading Gaol.
Wonders about prisoners on remand –
do they still look out through iron bars,
and treasure their little tent of blue?

Voices are buried in the town's earth.
Today they are spiralling, their words
are rubbing against stones and moss,
trying to climb to a circle of light.

Lads sit by the well, drinking beer
chucking in the odd can, and fags –
though one Midsummer's day,
someone placed rushes around the rim.

The Mole-God

I rushed in, dropped everything, read your note:
It said, 'I've gone to find out about the mole God.'
Then the phone went. When I'd finished talking,
I thought of you, setting off in your safari hat,
crawling through all those tunnels – then stopping,
wondering if you were looking in the right place,
if the ground above was mole-equivalent to sky.
Instead of clouds you'd gaze at trees or traffic lights.

I read the note again, this time turned the page:
It said, 'I've gone to find out about the mole God
put on my back! We'll need to talk about it later.'
I think you already know where the mole-god lives.
You're staring in its face. I wish you could've found
something brown and velvety, crowned with glory.

House Clearance

Time stepped from somewhere under the stairs.
They didn't seem to know he'd been waiting,
curled in brown paper at the back of pictures,
in the imperfections under layers of paint.
He scrawled in the dust between the banisters,
tiptoed to the window to watch the world drift.
Years passed and they noticed his stifled laughter
his cobwebbed hand reach for the light switch.

Now he's in the larder, with out-of-date cans
and mouldy pots of jam. 'Everything must go,'
he shouts – they don't hear him, they've shrunk
from the world that's flying past their window.
At last, it's their turn to slip between the boards,
weigh down the dust that lives beneath the floor.

Girl Bitten by Rat Outside McDonald's
– Picture

(billboard in Reading 2008)

An action shot of a girl and a rat,
we really must have a look at that.

Perhaps it'll be just a photo of the rat,
with staring eyes and bared teeth,
a mug shot with numbers underneath.
We really must have a look at that.

Was it a white rat or was it black,
or something somewhere in between?
A hoodie-type rat in low-slung jeans?
We really must have a look at that.

Or maybe the girl wound up the rat?
Perhaps she's fit, she took off her kit.
Yeah, we know she was asking for it.
We really must get a look at that

We got the paper, looked for the facts,
violence, animals, women, food,
what more could any one story hold?
We really must get a look at that.

We scanned through the paper
found the headline near the back:
Shock, horror, girl bitten by rat.
And the picture was of … McDonald's.

Nature Boy

He decided to live in the city.
When his mother came to stay
she said he'd changed.
The flossy hair on his head
had turned to stubble.
His eyes had frosted over.

As they walked in the street,
he couldn't hear the grit
shifting in the buildings,
or see the smashed-up
fossils and corals, glowing
red and orange in the walls.

Not for him the under-wing
of the evening; or the diligent
zigzags of passers-by,
coming from their offices.
She left him fixed to a bench,
a statue in a sculpture trail.

She would think of him
as a young man, standing in
the speckled night sky,
his arms spreading outwards,
as the pulp of former lives
swelled-up inside him.

Bye, Bye Baby

He hurtled out of the ward's green doors –
they flapped and spluttered like sucker fish
falling from the side of a liner in dry dock.

He poked his head back in for a moment;
the doors opened as much as a clam does.

'I want my freedom,' he shouted at me.
I lay there, staring at his polished-floor face.

As if freedom was something I snipped at
with scissors, grown blunt over time from
cutting people down to the size of minnows.

I said, 'We all need responsibilities, maybe
they're the only things that keep us sane.'

And the doors flopped shut and shuddered.
An imagined tender core quivered once
then meandered out from a crushed pearl.

'Trust me,' the nurse said, 'you won't feel a thing.'

Lesley Saunders

I have lived in Slough – ten minutes' bike ride and I'm on the Thames towpath at Eton – for most of my adult life. I've also studied in Oxford and worked in London, so (though without my being consciously aware of it until now) the waters of the Thames have flowed through my life.

'Garden' and 'Grace' each came about through my connection with Oxford, whose geography and ecology have been shaped by the rivers Isis and Cherwell and the Oxford canal. Many of the other poems in this selection – 'Lure', 'Face', 'Aubade', 'Serenade' and 'Chinese Mitten Crab' – have their origin in the series of one-day workshops brilliantly designed and led over several years by Jane Draycott at the River and Rowing Museum in Henley-on-Thames. After giving us lots of literary stimuli, Jane would send us out to wander through the museum or sit by the river and write: the combination of mentor and setting seemed to release our creative energies: perhaps the river at Henley has that particular sense of paciness as well as amplitude that is conducive to the imagination? Certainly many of us went on to publish pieces that were first drafted there.

The image of water as a great welter of elemental force had been sloshing round in my mind for a good few years, since a holiday on the dramatic Atlantic coast of northern Spain. It suddenly found poetic form in June 2010 when two performance artists, Ann Rapstone and Hilary Kneale, took a residency at Turbine House, which spans the River Kennet in the centre of Reading. They had the idea of inviting local poets to come along and read something on the theme of water and rivers. Kate Noakes (another Two Rivers poet) and I visited them at work a week before our joint performance on the open day: their installation/performance in that unique location was emotionally moving as well as intriguing and very inventive. And then I found myself able to write the poem that I called 'Even in England'.

I first became involved with Two Rivers Press when Peter Hay designed and published – and produced a wonderful series of images for *Christina the Astonishing*, which Jane Draycott and I wrote together in the late 1990s. Then a decade later Two Rivers (under the guidance of John Froy) published another collaboration, *Her Leafy Eye*, in which my poems inspired by the 18th century gardens at Rousham in Oxfordshire were complemented by the images of Geoffrey Carr; 'Rill' is from that collection. The excellent – and instantly recognizable – quality of production that Two Rivers Press has consistently accomplished is one of its many strengths: books made to be held in the hand and mind as beautiful objects …

Even in England

Even in England you can be woken by the earth's
heave underneath you, the tremor and flood
of uncovered memories.

>   It was not like that.

The room and its darknesses jutted out like a rock,
we floated away on the water's breathing, the rise
and fall of each other's sighs,

>   the night-long tide,

and between us and our dreams, the tireless turbines
of moon-driven welter grinding the world to stones.
Brushing our teeth in the morning

>   we were lost in the blue.

Back in the house a faulty tap has been dripping for days.
The bowl in the sink is overflowing, its silvering rim
like a weir leaking a lake,

>   wet finding its levels.

But we, we seek the source.

Garden

'In play we transform the world according to our desires'
Jerome Bruner

Today I am cloud-minded, bookish, my pages illumined
by this lichenish leaf-sieved light. Time is the artist here.
What you can see from the dark-eyed rooms of your tree-house

is child's play, look, a lawn of shadows, quick accomplices
in the planting of ancestral wychwood, a sarsen under the stars,
a park bench in the sun. My students are effortlessly disciplined

in the greening of stories, finding new eye-rhymes for dwelling.
Here. Sit with me. *In the trees birds of paradise are calling.*

*Commissioned for the garden at Oxford University Department
of Education*

Face

'One thinks of the practice of blackening the teeth. Might it not
have been an attempt to push everything except the face into the dark?'
Junichiro Tanizaki, *In Praise of Shadows*

I am pushing everything
    into the dark but your face
is the moon rising through water.

Everything is pushing us
    into the dark but I am holding
on to your face between my hands.

The dark is pushing me
    down past the water but your face
is already a scull plunging deeper.

Serenade

Not knowing how close the bank is, how far away the edge,
  you stand stockstill in your sleep, seeing in the seam
of your eye or room the crack of light between curtains, trees,
  the full beam of a car in the far distance winging away

to its elsewhere, a night-chafer nearing and gone, tunnelling
  into the silence, then a long moment later a detonation
at the margins of darkness that shakes the fields like a plane
  passing too close to a windowpane or a thief breaking in

at the back. The night closes in like a bend in the river. It is
  not to be spoken to. It is waiting for the next thing to happen:
you down by the weir watching your dayself the passenger
  not knowing how far away the bank is, how close the edge.

Aubade

This morning I am all conjecture,
   I did not wake like a bather
      rising clean and clear out of water

resting at the edge in the sun to dry.
   No, the river is a long deep hollowed-out breath
      I am breathing to stay down,

not to hear what it is the rooks are saying
   not to be brushed by the hot-faced hawthorn
      on the path that leads only to afternoon.

I am pulling the chilled river closer to me
   with an effort huge as sleep, I am holding
      the bones of the river in my arms

but that deafening sound is the birds on its banks
   and the hawthorn burns like an awakening.

Grace

For what you are about to receive is something broken
    that needs no mending: the daily loaves of give and take,
the elementary etiquette of harvest and its common wealth.

For what you are about to walk through is a portal
    that needs no password, a door you found already open,
an arch joined at the fingertips or your face lit by a rainbow.

For what you are about to learn by heart is a library
    that needs no deciphering, its leaves shining with questions
like a great feast laid out for you on the high table of summer.

Yet in some future winter carved of wood and stone and sky,
    in the quiet refectory of its evening, every windowpane a wall
of dark and the garden still as glass, you may find yourself

toasting the old hunter-gatherers, how once they were encased
    bone by bone here: praise-singers, full of strangeness, grace.

*Commissioned to mark the opening in June 2009 of the new
dining facilities at Kellogg College at 60 Banbury Road, Oxford.
The building previously housed part of the Pitt-Rivers
ethnological collection.*

Chinese Mitten Crab

This is my last self, hard-backed

        and landlocked

refugee from my body's past

        its soft-celled children

I glued together out of wet sand

        and wide grey skies

grieving as they bobbed goodbye

        goodbye.

I became a goddess of the old kind

        the ones

whose filthiness is in their skirts

        who do not perish

on their wedding nights.

        Our bad habits sap

the teetering virtues of cities

        parked on riverbanks

– oh here comes the landslip

        the night-soil

the arse-over-tit the scree

        of secrets and dowries

crash it goes, crash and I am

        your underself always

just out of sight keeping you company

        as you sink

as low as you can get. I am not made opal

        by the moon

I do not recall what is meant by

        chrysanthemum.

Look these are my stillborns my widow-weeds

        my cabinet

of curiosities my terracotta army.

        My servant-mourners.

Rill

Water's fickle. Its uncalled-for free-fall
    over mangroves and patios fills

the monsoon afternoons with grand pianos,
    a flash-flood of fishes, the slapstick

of mudflats: lucky for some. A bucket or well
    will hold a week of sky close as milk

but a sleeve of silk is thirst from shoulder
    to wrist, water runs through its weave

like blood in a vein, its one unbroken thread
    bright as a road, tall and taut as a fell.

Left out in the sun, a land burns to saltpans
    and dustbowls, hands empty of gifts.

Like caliphs we wait for the snowmelt, first
    seep of spring in the ditch, its skeins

of wet felting the stones under mulberry, myrtle,
    till all we hear is this hurtle of newborns,

the clean clear voices of *acequias, alcantarillas,*
    the paddling scarlet feet of partridge chicks.

David Cooke

Philip Larkin, in his sardonic reworking of Thomas Hood's poem 'I Remember, I Remember', describes how, passing through Coventry on a train, he suddenly remembered it was the place where he was born. After sketching out key moments in a life he might have lived, but didn't, he comes to the sad conclusion that 'Nothing, like something, happens anywhere.' For me, Reading is the town where I grew up in the 1950s and 1960s and where, unlike Larkin, I can see now that I more or less became the person I am. The eldest of four children, I was born into a family that was Irish and Roman Catholic. Like so many of their contemporaries, my parents had come to this country from the West of Ireland in the hope of finding a better life. With a bare minimum of education they had plenty of 'nous' and a determination to get on. Meeting up in North London when my mum was sixteen and my dad was in his twenties, they married two years later. Then, in 1952, the year before I was born, they moved from London to Reading, a place that my mother at first hated after the buzz and excitement of Camden Town. Nevertheless, by the time I had any sense of what was going on around me my parents were well integrated into a lively and extensive Irish community whose principal focus was the Catholic Church. During the week the young women would meet up at the Mothers' Union, whilst the men, in time-honoured tradition, would scuffle through Sunday Mass and then slope off for a 'session' in the pub before returning home for lunch.

Reading, crucially, is also the place where I went to school. My primary school was St James's situated in that amazing patch of ground surrounded by the ruins of the great medieval Abbey, the Forbury Gardens, and Reading Gaol. Our teachers, again almost exclusively Irish or of Irish descent, left us in little doubt about who the 'good guys' and the 'bad guys' were in history and made sure we knew about the sacrifices that had been made in our name. I doubt if these days eight and nine year olds are quite as well informed as we were about hanging and quartering or being burnt at the stake. From St. James's I moved on to Presentation College, a Roman Catholic grammar school for boys, where I was taught by the Christian Brothers and drilled remorselessly on Latin declensions, dates, the Periodic Table. I have to admit that the Brothers were nifty with a cane if you didn't toe the line and were always obsessed with the length of our hair. Still, I think we mostly survived and did get a sound education for which I'm grateful. Childhood may, ultimately, be no more than a myth we reinvent inside our heads. At least, I suspect that mine is, since the Reading that I knew as a kid is now a ghostly palimpsest that doesn't exist in the real world. So much of it was bulldozed flat years ago and 'redeveloped'. Nevertheless, for better or worse, I think it has made me who I am.

Shadow Boxing

The closest my dad ever got to poetry
was when he savoured some word
like *pugilist*, or the tip-toe springiness
he sensed in *bob and weave*,
his unalloyed delight in the flytings
and eyeball to eyeball hype
that went with big fight weigh-ins.

And I too might have been
a contender when I did my stint
in the ring, my dad convinced
I had style and the stamp of a winner,
when in the end I just got bored.
You had to have a killer's instinct,
to do much better than a draw.

In the gym the lights are low.
It's after hours. I'm on my own.
The boards are rank with sweat
and stale endeavour. Shadow boxing
like the best of them, I will show
him feints, a classic stance,
trying always to keep up my guard.

Faith of our Fathers

The creed we'd inherited, it was unambiguous
and always claimed us as its own
in a far-fetched calculus of chances.
Aspersion and charms
were tokens of our election.

And when our foreheads
were smudged with ash, it taught us
the word *mortality*, like a chapel
I've seen in my afterlife
built with cement and bones.

At the age of reason
peccadillos stamped with guilt
could be absolved in a box of whispers,
and purity of thought
reinforced in threadbare rituals,

spreading over our lives
a drab brocade.
Behind it all were generations
who had prayed like us and chanted,
professing faith in our creed.

Sustained by desperation and the certainty
that human ties will cease,
they had sought continuance,
their dreamscapes
shimmering through isolation.

A Wet Break

Outside in the street where skies have opened
a dingy curtain flaps across the day,
as rain beats down with blank persistence
on shining roofs of cars, dissolves
my windowpanes, reminding me now
for no apparent purpose of a wet break
at primary school, how in partitioned rooms
with raggedy copies of *Beano* or *Dandy*,
we were fractious *Bash Street Kids*
with time enough to spare; and if an hour
seemed stuck forever in a non-event
of walls and rain, years have since
spun free, cruising blurred distances,
adjusted to the focus of each idle glance.

The House on Orchard Street

A three-up two-down end terrace, its door
opening onto the street, my dad had paid for it
cash down, then filled it up with wrecks –
a seemingly hand-picked gang of failures,
who let the bookies collect his rent.
My mother mopped its cracked linoleum,
unable to sweeten air that reeked
of dodgy fry-ups and dubious sheets.

When the Department for Highways claimed it
its lease had long expired. With somewhere to go
a flyover soars above its levelled site.

St James Primary

I'm working back to the dreamtime
of St. James Primary in sixty-three,
the occluded and innocent days
before the gadgets and money took over –

like trying to retrieve the original colours
of bright, ridged slabs of plasticine
from muddied clumps we used
for *project work* in the afternoons –

my finest effort the model I made
with Terence O'Neill of the Martyrdom
of Hugh Cook Faringdon
that earned us two gold stars.

In our tiny enclave we were swamped
by history: a Victorian church,
where we crocodiled to mass on Wednesdays,
interceding for the re-conversion of Russia;

and the airy, abandoned carcase
of an abbey that kept the secret
of a good king's bones,
its wrecked clerestories hoarding space.

Boys and girls, we never discovered
the mysteries of the others' playground,
but chanted tables daily –
our paean to the god of rote learning.

Money

What is it about money and the mystery
of where it comes from that takes me back again
to a clipped patrician voice and the lesson
my parents had scarcely needed to learn
when, reinventing the meaning
of home, they knew already
they had never had it so good?

For nigglesome years I bridled
at having to learn the value of money –
its grudging laws that set you free;
yet still admit to admiration
for the gangling tea boy my dad had been
when he pocketed hopeless bets,
working on the railways.

My dad could always tell you a tale
about a fool and his money
with the unassailable knowingness
he'd earned as a self-made man
and didn't need a politician
to tell him more half-truths
about *his* pound in his pocket.

Mischief

I was prelapsarian and just curious.
I couldn't tell you the price of anything,

my jackdaw eyes twitching
at a glint of silver between the floorboards.

And later on there were camps and dens,
private worlds, like one I built

with a clean sheet and a clothes horse
traipsed across the grass

and filled up with treasure –
the lodger's flashy cuff links,

of which one, suddenly pointless,
survived and sent my mother

on a hopeless quest. At the back
of the yard was a lock-up

raised on piles. It offered a space
that seemed appropriate

for my discovery of fire.
The flames were impish blues and yellows

that rose up triumphantly before me.
To this day my mother can laugh.

She calls me her *Antichrist*.
God knows how I ever survived.

Soap

When the days were out of kilter
between the daylight and the dark
our mother set a limit:
7.30 and bed, a watershed
marked twice weekly
by the funereal brass that drifted
off *Coronation Street*,
its title sequence disappearing
into a Land of Nod
beyond terraced roofs.

Trailing upstairs
to functional bedrooms,
we mumbled slipshod prayers,
before plunging, breathless,
into chilly sheets …

Late one night
I am dreaming voices –
a woman still young,
who has her brood, and a man
who is buoyed by pub talk,
the *craic*, his cronies …

Her litany is a wall
he won't get past, until he, too,
has learned that patience has its limits.

Caversham

The wrought-iron gates
of its cemetery
swing open and shut
in the memory now like pages

of a dreary book.
They guard a barren
secret, genteel lawns and boughs.
It's there the chosen lie

in the acre we leased
from God, beside Ukrainians,
Poles, Italians.
Time since has made me

a stranger to kin
I accompanied there,
and souls whose terminal
progress filled mornings

free from school –
yet still I recall that shared
unease at the spectre
of others' grief.

The Forbury Gardens

Through a side gateway whose unassuming
frame is draped in swags of pale wisteria
like hairstyles worn by Victorian girls,
I return to a half-remembered space,
its neat enclosure more clearly defined
by flint walls than the past will ever be;

and where parched lawns, diminished and threadbare
in the unseasonable heat, mark out
a territory that can't now be repossessed –
the tiny fortress of Forbury Hill,
the bandstand's lookout, and the benched refuge
we reinvented as a secret cave.

Today even the Lion towering above
his plinth seems at a loss to justify
those fallen in Afghan wars, staring,
muscle-bound, into a sky where cranes loll,
ponderingly, raising disposable
futures from a debris of junked decades.

Like vague impulsive ghosts, those earlier selves
who rampaged in drab, unfashionable
clothes, our echoes trapped as a sibilance
in the tunnel that brought us, crash landing,
onto holy ground: a ruined abbey's
lost domain of ritual and trauma.

Hagiography and a dead language
bound us to our past, the tedium also
of a Corpus Christi parade winding
slowly through these gardens, the air heavy
with hymns and incense, my tired head mesmerised
by a thurible clattering against its chains.

Jean Watkins

Originally from Yorkshire, I have lived just north of Reading for many years. In 2001, as a mature student, I gained a BA in English from the University of Reading. Afterwards I studied creative writing at the School of Continuing Education. I attend poetry classes and workshops and am a regular listener and open-mic contributor at Reading Poets' Café.

'In Reading' arose from the drive round the Forbury in the evening rush hour on my way to a workshop run by Peter Robinson at Reading Library. The poem was very little altered after the workshop although it is unusual for me to produce an almost complete poem at one sitting.

'Thames' was the result of a sonnet workshop given by Jo Shapcott at the River and Rowing Museum as part of the Henley Literature Festival in 2007. After bombarding us with fascinating facts and brilliant examples Jo suggested that we should write Bouts-Rimés sonnets. The end words are decided in advance and the poem has to fit round them.

'Rower, Moulsford' was triggered partly by my familiarity with the towpath and Brunel's railway bridge at Moulsford, and partly from a visit to the Museum of English Rural Life. Here I saw an exhibition about people whose work is connected to the river. One of the photographs was of this man and below it were some of his reflections on his relationship with the river.

'What will survive of us' is also set on the Thames. As usual, different strands twisted into this poem: my interest in archaeology, collages at the River and Rowing Museum made from assorted articles found in the river, and the idea of writing a list poem.

'Lock Keeper's Daughter' reflects the contrasting moods of the river. It can seem like a malign beast during a raging flood, and in 1982 it swept the Shiplake lock keeper to his death. Local newspapers were full of the event and I know the site well. I wrote the poem from the point of view of an imaginary daughter who revisits the lock many years later.

'Jilted Lover, Jealous Wife': headlines were also generated by this shocking murder. Emily Salvini, aged 8, died in an arson attack at her home in Caversham in May 1997. Her mother

Katherine and 3 year-old brother Zach survived. I was transfixed by the juxtaposition of hatred and innocence, and the pathos of her death.

'Scrimshaw' was quite an early poem and was my attempt to convey the appeal of collecting. It reflects my own interest in a variety of antiques and the stories behind them

In Reading

Big letters QTR on the orange articulated lorry
edging its way round the Forbury. Russet leaves
of horse chestnuts haloed by evening sun.

Reflections on plate glass windows with posters
SALE SALE in red. Exhaust fumes smoking,
a vapour trail snailing across the blue.

High walls lock in the prison, reach up
at the abbey, with space for grass and sky.
A ghostly crescent moon above the Kennet

confined in its concrete bed. It slinks under
the IDR, dull brown with dull brown Canada geese
and crayfish hiding in another world.

Thames

For years our waste had fouled the river scene
scumming the water, bringing disarray
to banks, where voles and otters haven't been
able to hunt or fish in their past way.
A stinking effluent sullied every leaf
dropped by the trees, and those who looked for old
artefacts, shovelling mud into a sieve
found gobs of oil and plastic bottles, stalled
in creeks and backwaters. Herons which flew
with heavy flaps were gone, but now they loom
out of the river's mist and morning's dew.
The stickleback builds his nest like a cocoon
in water alpine clean. What I mistook
for dead is living: salmon leap beside each lock.

Rower, Moulsford

Under Brunel's skewed bridge his skiff
looks liquid, spills into reflections.
Slant courses of bricks clone the slope
of his oar, the white line on his Lycra sheath.

He had tried not to rouse the river
seeming asleep in its gunmetal grey.
Strove for the perfect stroke to stroke
its surface, soothe its skin, not break
into its dreams. The sun crept up
to his eye-line, infused the water,
thawed the ache from his icy hands.

Some days islands of sediment swirl
downstream, wheeling like shoals
of fish. Driftwood leviathans threaten
his out-reach oars. His boat ploughs
choppy waves, cross-eddies; skims
like an insect over upside-down sky.

What Will Survive of Us

Slowly, as the tide turned,
the river began to seep away,
grudgingly giving up its mudbanks.
Then in wellingtons or waders
they went down with shovels,
buckets, trowels, plastic bags;
struggled through sucking mud,
shoved in sharp blades and found
broken clay pipes, rubber gloves,
pieces of willow-pattern crockery,
a doll's body with one leg, one arm;
a cog wheel, a green glass bottle
bubble-beaded; and when a spade
grated through gravel, an old gold
poesy ring engraved inside:
Life long our love goeth on.

Jilted Lover, Jealous Wife

The person must have worn dark clothing
picked a moonless night, carried a bag
with wire cutters, a length of hose
and petrol can. They must have moved
down the road like a shadow, hooded,
soft-shoed. What white-hot hatred
made them cut the telephone wire,
pour petrol through the letterbox,
apply the match? Did they watch,
make sure the door was well alight
paint blistering, flames licking and smoke
exploring the porch, before they crept away?
Or perhaps they hid nearby, to hear
the mother's screams, fire-engine siren;
watch firemen on ladders carrying
two children and the mother down.
Helped to an ambulance, they would be
coughing up smoke, except for Emily,
eight, who by that time was dead.

Lock Keeper's Daughter

Even now, when I can't sleep, I hear
those howling trees, rain hurled
at windows, the river's manic surge.
Dad went to open the straining gates,
was gulped, digested, husk spewed
into reeds a mile downstream.

Today I thread through Friesians on the towpath.
Stick-insect double scullers barely ruffle
the river's glaze, mirroring the willows.
Our house is white now and the garden blooms
with tables, sun umbrellas. Wasps buzz
round jam dishes, swallows still unzip the sky.

Scrimshaw

It started with Aunt Ellen's sperm whale tooth
scored with wooden ships, sails bulging
like washday sheets. In the curvy lines of waves
whales spout water, flick their tails.

I have others now, showing sailors in the rigging,
doll-like couples hand in hand in gardens.
A baleen stay busk with cottage, church and castle
was once warmed by her skin when he was far away.

I hold them and sense rope-callused hands
scratching with a jack knife, the thumb
smoothing in lamp-black. A stench of blood and blubber
in his nostrils, he gouges an arrow piercing a heart.

A. F. Harrold

I live in Reading by mistake. Most of the decisions I've made in my life have been happy mistakes of that sort. I grew up in Horsham, a small Sussex market town, and came here to study philosophy at the university. It wasn't my first choice and I'd never visited when I put it down as my insurance offer. I failed to get the grades to go where I wanted and failed to get the marks for here either, but my sixth form tutor spoke to someone in the department and then phoned me and said, 'Ashley, you're going to Reading.' That was the autumn of 1993 and I'm still here.

I find it difficult to believe that place has any particular bearing on what I write. As far as I can tell I'd be writing the same sort of things whether I lived in Reading, LA or Didcot. That is to say, I would be writing poems like the poems I write now – essentially inward facing lyrics, notes of small occurrences indoors, metaphysical squibs. There is little or no *genius loci* to these.

I pay poor attention to bricks, to the streets or the parks. They are just the places around me, but not of me. I feel little bond with them, no fond affection, no Proustian need to remember them. I don't feel an especially meaningful relationship with the place.

Of course the specific poems I have written grew from my being here in this particular place, because it is here that I have many of my experiences, here that I have most of my friends, here that my daily relationships play out. Had I gone back to Horsham after I graduated and stayed there, none of that would exist. To be honest, I can't imagine what I could have done in that nice small town. For one thing, I would know none of the people I know now, and they're far more important than geography or architecture – one's true location is as a nexus in a web of relationships, and I have living in Reading to thank for the precise blend the last two decades have provided. The second thing I have Reading to thank for, is that by being here I fell, by further mistakes, coincidences and misadventures, into the arms of Two Rivers Press. Some years ago I ended up taking

over the reins of Poets' Café from Susan Utting. But years
before that she, and others at Poets' Café and Thin Raft, gave me
a platform and advice and encouragement for the poetry I was
writing in the last years of the last century. Now I'm continuing
her work in providing a platform to both the old guard and the
new generation of poets from the region. That small thing is
probably the most important contribution I have to make to
Reading's thriving poetry scene, and I'm very pleased to be
making it.

Swan-Road Sketch

Envious of the world, I stand by the long way,
grey-slate silver-black pattered with drizzle,
and watch the lordly lazy white long-neck
make his lomping lazy lope along that road,
neck straight out, wings wide as Viking sails.

Too slow, he seems to go, so too damn slow,
treading the water as if he weren't that weighty,
meaty, mighty muscle-feather of river-king,

but then, triumphally silent, he beats, lifts
and arm-wrestles the wind under his wing,
outruns the sticky dull meniscus gravity
and before my very eyes, *good god!*, there he is,
a free-flying, flame-white arrow in flight.

Lyric: How Long This Night Is

(*a version after the Middle English*)

The summer nights, starting late
and ending with the rose-lit chorus
of unseen birds, sprightly, awake
and eager, were short and merry ones.

But now storms have fallen on us,
soon frost will leak out of the leaves,
and my matching grief-loaded loss
lengthens all future nights interminably.

Snail, Silver Street

Uphill. Single-footed step by step,
each contiguous to the last, stretching forwards
as you tip back for the next wriggling haul up.
Proudly centred on the grey-grit pavement,
following in the direction of pedestrians,
oblivious to the perils I see – having faith
that such things as will be simply will be.
I pause to watch you, crouch. Uphill, wriggling
with that focussed perfect shell, curling in,
300 million years of design shining out,
you plough on, a singular muscle shifting stone.
Those twin pinhead black eyeballs
fluctuate inside the pinnacle stalks, sway toward me,
decide I am nothing much, sway away and you
plough on, up this hill with a hundred yards
of lifetime concrete pavement to pass
before you reach a place
much the same as where you are now.

The Noise

It can be such a quiet thing, death.

Fanfares, explosions, coughs, cries – yes.

Or a stillness, resolving like a film's
cross-fade into a stiller silence. A settling
of sheets, breath, sunlight. A quiet affair.

Outside Now

Pigeons the size of dodos
are wading – wings wide,
chests as entirely ruffled
as all Elizabethan possibilities –
are paddling in the puddled pools
that lake across the flat roof
outside my window.

Two of them stop their bathing,
stand all prinked out
like startled puffer-fish,
cock an eye each in my direction.

I step nearer the window,
smile at their swollen size,
wish for them to stay, to carry on,
but seeing me and suddenly shy
they pull on their coats,
do up their buttons,
look like pigeons everywhere.

On Not Being St Hildegard

I'd say this headache has come back, except
that's a continuity I can't claim.
It felt like this last night: a dry, burst hum.

I wonder if it's, perhaps, a tumour in there,
pressing itself as it shifts in the neuron stew;
or maybe it's too much sun, tv or thinking.

Like a seed or stone or slug it is selfish –
sometimes it waits in the morning, a mallet
leant on my frontal lobe as I wake;
other days it's afternoons. Now, it's night.

One day I'll find out what it's always been
(if it turns out to be anything) by accident –
as a footnote aside to some quite other exam.

It comes and goes, but it's just a headache,
after all. It doesn't spin me visions
or voices; I see no cities, angels or answers.

Human Beings Saying Human Words

It can be the smallest thing that makes me happy:
take that train guard on that train leaving Oxford
ten minutes late, just last Thursday, who hoped
that *with a fair set of sails and a good tail wind*
we might make up some time and perhaps, even,
reach Reading just five minutes behind schedule.

And he reminded me of that Amtrak guard,
who so brilliantly said, when the train stopped
at the third or fourth unexpected red signal,
already forty minutes late on course for LA,
that we *might as well just throw the schedule away* –
not a phrase he learnt on the training course –

and he went on speaking, finger on the button,
tannoy speculating on both floors of the train,
to tell the story of some chap he'd followed,
a famous NASCAR driver who won and won
and then one day lost, who, when accosted
by journalists eagerly snapping for petulance

or tears, just shrugged and said *sometimes, you know,
you just don't win.* And there we were, stuck,
looking out at the Pacific rolling in the sunshine
and I thought that these two were the good guys,
those left who still believe they guard passengers,
not customers, and who care enough to say so.

Houseplants

I am almost always a helpless killer of houseplants.
When my obituary gets written it won't read –
the poet, who died peacefully in the bath last night,
is survived by three aspidistra and a succulent.
No – they will have gone on long before me.

I'm led to believe it may be an inherited trait –
my nan never received flowers for long.
She gave away growing gifts as soon as
the generous givers were out of the room.
My mother took them in – they grew for her.

I suffer an addictive personality – in short bursts.
Sudden enthusiasms erupt and wither with time –
what filled my days, mind and hands soon goes –
the love affair runs out of steam, the steamer sits
filling a corner of the kitchen dry and silent.

Poor plants though – taken in always in good faith
and overwatered liberally for a few quick weeks –
they wilt with my indulgence, my diligence, my care,
but how else, I ask, can I show them my love?
Like flannels they droop, look sick, and I feel guilt,

promise to give them space, and soon do just that.
Passing through the living room one day, I notice
a stick drop its last yellow leaf into a pot of dry earth –
and I apologize, feel the guilt twist, but run outside
to where my new friend sits waiting in her new car.

Summer Neglect

Things go on growing in her garden,
but order decays. Borders grow old
and ragged, grow green. Thorny arms
reach out for ledges, for hands to hold.

Colour fades as leafy things spring up.
The odd hold out grows rare. Thinking
gives way to nature. The pond evaporates,
a damp ring-mark on stones, daily sinking.

Susan Utting

Reading, poetry and Two Rivers are forever linked for me. Reading is where I first found my feet (or should that be 'voice') as a poet at Thin Raft Poetry Group and had my first small successes with a prize at the Reading Literature Festival in 1993, followed by a collaborative pamphlet with artist Peter Hay, Two Rivers Press founder.

Rivers do seem to provide marvellous metaphors for poets and for the writing of poems: the urgent push to write, the relentless struggle to keep going, then the rush when it's going well and the delight at having got there in the end – a process I've tried to embody in 'The Poem That Wanted To Be A River'. I am very aware of the power and the potential dangers of rivers, a respect I learned from my father, who was a skilful sailor and who frequently crops up in my poems. He's there in 'Altering The Clocks' and conspicuously *not* there to save my mother from the flood in the extract from 'My Mother's House'. My parents retired to Reading from the Midlands, and my father felt very much at home here because of his closeness to the Thames and its tributaries. He was born on the coast and also loved the sea, so to make up for the fact that he is now buried 'inland' in a Wokingham churchyard, I wrote 'Flood' to take him on an imaginary journey by way of the Thames back to his original home, the sea.

Reading is the place where my life as a working poet really began. I graduated in English at Reading University in 1993 and began teaching creative writing there and on various Arts Council residencies. 'The Rules of Frisbee' is set in a Creative Writing Fellowship workshop on the University Campus, and '12 Months On' was commissioned by the Reading Evening Post on the first anniversary of the Paddington rail disaster, as part of my stint as Year of the Artist Community Laureate. It was a difficult commission to fulfil, but one I was proud to be asked to attempt.

I've lived all over England – by the time I was 30 I had moved more than 20 times – so have always been perplexed

by or resistant to the notion of *home*. 'Where are you from?'
is a difficult question for me, but it's one I've often tried to
answer in poems, as in 'Catechism', which has become something
of a signature poem. Then, after a stay on the east coast at
Aldeburgh, feeling at the end of a productive and enjoyable week
that I was more than ready to 'go home', I knew exactly where
that was. I had lived in Berkshire longer than anywhere else
in my life and was ready to admit that this was the place, if not
exactly where I came from, nevertheless the place I wanted
to go back to. I realized that 'Going Home' really did mean
back to my own small corner of the Thames Valley.

The poem that wanted to be a river

squeezed itself like water
through a narrow channel,

dark, fishless at first, it was a trickle,
a stranger to light, air, movement.

Slowly, as it grew used to the sound
of itself, its glug and gurgle began

to please it, so it carried on, turned
feisty, so full of itself it gushed a flood,

pushed rock, shale, mud aside, spewed
silt to banks, forced living things

from its bed, its root, became
a living thing itself. In its wordy rush

to light, air, movement, sound,
the poem was shameless, was a river.

Flood

The lawn is a lake and still it comes down,
it lashes and sluices down gutter and glass,
the yard in an eddy of flowerheads and dross
and I am reminded of stories of sand bags
stacked on a river bank, four deep, ten high,
the unstoppable Ouse, lost fortunes and lives,
bulb fields and orchards, whole nurseries of glass
swept along, swept away in the rush to the sea.

I'm reminded of building a boat, watching
my father at work, inland and steady, doggedly
dreaming of seashores and oceans whilst making
a fresh water Fireball, his racer for reservoirs,
gravel pit Sundays, his stop gap for sea fever;
and my single-sailed dinghy, easy to handle, a Foil
for a learner, wind ignorant, nervous of water,
he made it for me *uncapsizable, safer than land.*

I'm reminded of church yards and graves,
of ashes to ashes and dust, and the waterlogged
ground, the bones of the dead in the ground,
my father there, inland and rain wet, dreaming
of salt; dreaming of floodwaters reaching his bones
sweeping them out of their grave in a river of mud,
rushing them out to the road, through the streets
and estates, past houses with lawns that are lakes,

over the common to Riverside Walk, into the Emm,
to the Loddon and on to the Thames, all the way
down to the estuary, back in a rush to the sea.

Catechism

'What is your Name?
Who gave you this Name?
What did your Godfathers and Godmothers then for you?'

I come from a place with *beech* in its name;
my name then was wished for, dropped
from the mouth of an old woman, fat
as a grandmother, soft, round as an egg.

Conceived in the eye of a sad man,
I was born at the trip of a young woman's
foot, a tumble that rushed me, unready
to air, light, gravity's chill.

I was nourished on milk from the tip
of a spoon, sugar-sweet, thickened
with bread; and crucible tops from soft-
boiled eggs, made yellow, salty with butter.

I grew fat, white as a grub, gurgled,
babbled, spoke, settled for serious talk.
Loquacious, prodigious, I figured the world
in my mouth, made language a loose tooth

to push with my tongue – *cylinder, Hollander,
colander, kiosk* – I rolled it around,
five years without stopping for breath.
I gorged on its sweet, salt, bitter, sour,

sucked hard on it, bloodied the roof
of my mouth with its acid. I come from
the quiet of a coy girl, dark-eyed, slim
at the waist, a girl in a green dress,

whose name then was chosen by men,
who taught her to lower her eyes, press
her lips, narrow her throat, swallow words
down; who taught me the power of *hush, hush, hush.*

Altering the Clocks

This is not the time for falling back
to thoughts of the dying of bees,
of fathers, sisters, daughters, held
by a steady thread of prayer, mouthed
or hummed in the heads of unbelievers.

We have passed the danger days,
the anniversaries of the *one sure thing*
and reached the time to spring forward
into the light of afternoons, their growing
warm, to the tips of green things that will

push up through the mud, we know they will
unfurl themselves, like memories of the dead
they'll come again; at the altering of clocks
we reach the safe time, move closer to believers.

from My Mother's House

All night she's dreamt of rowing boats, the heads of dogs
and flotsam bobbing down the street, bedraggled cats
with arched and shivering backs stuck high on rooftops.

She climbs a chair to look out of her window: not a sign
of paving stone or tarmac, the pillar box has gone, the shop
across the street starts two floors up with residential nets.

She watches shaky mirror pictures in a dirty river, tries
to stare them still, to fix them there – *no nearer, higher,
closer* – loses to a kitchen stool that floats past on its side.

She climbs down to a dead phone, a double-bolted door,
no peephole to see out of, to see in through, a muffled
knocker and a disconnected bell. Upstairs, she's safe –

the only safe one left until they come, as come they will,
tramping higher, nearer, closer till they find her there.
She listens; then starts to drag the chair across the room

towards the door, the bolts, the lock, the handle,
imagining its stiffness, the creak of unused hinges,
the draught, the crack of light that might come in.

The Rules of Frisbee

Let it be sunny, a Wednesday,
February, two hours after noon
when the frost has gone wet,
steamed off to a mirage of heat-haze.

Sit at a desk, in a row, in a room
(face the window), a room full of
heads down and listen. Hear the
scritching of pens, the shush-

shushing of graphite, watch
the sprint across A4 of ballpoint
and rollerball. Put down your pen,
tilt back your chair, jaunty,

clasp your hands at the back
of your head, elbows akimbo
and daydream, drift with the scene
in the frame of the window,

the open-air ballet of thrower to
catcher, catcher to thrower, leaping
like stars at the skim of the light-
hearted discus. Let it be sunny.

Twelve Months On

Commissioned by Reading Evening Post, *5th October 2000*
for the first anniversary of the Paddington Rail Disaster

Twelve months down the line there are
no flowers left alive from then, no wire
wall for messages, no place for poetry
or prayers among the shopfronts.

The coffee-croissant book and snack stalls
look the same, the Travellers' Fare's unchanged,
still there, the concourse pavement tables,
the commuter rush, the usual inter-city crush.

No sign of anything amiss, twelve months on
you'd never know; until you catch the eye
of someone who knew someone, somebody
who'd waited, who still waits, uncomforted

by poetry, knowing now that messages, like prayers
and mobile phones, are sometimes left unanswered.

Going Home

'Home is not where I come from;
home is where I'm going.'

Scuffed by the swoop of gulls,
shifty with ripples, grey as the grey
of an overcast sky, this morning's sea
is preoccupied with nothing more
than the noisy to-and-fro of itself.

Home slips from my lips without thought:
the fit of an odd number, the ring
of the name of a street, chosen
years ago now, known even then
without learning. There have been arms

like that, warm bodies, easy and close
as my own interlaced fingers.
This morning the sea is a stranger,
another's salt on my skin,
an unfamiliar address that disturbs

thought, that interrupts sleep
with its breathing. I'm moving away
from this noisy shore, inland, back
to the steady to-and-fro of myself,
back to brick, blossom, tarmac, bud,

click and shiver, skitter and creak,
to the comfort of sounds in the night
that I'll know like the sound of my
own heart in my ear, that I'll know
well enough not to hear, not to listen for.

Learning To Read

She remembered her first time, top deck of the bus,
a spiral of stripes on a pole, and *Barber's Shop*
see-sawed itself to her tongue, came out as a sing-
song of *baa baa sheep*, close but a fumble. Then
clap hands, she got it! Soon they were everywhere,
easy as peasy, shapes for the taking, into her head,
out through her mouth in oceans of hisses, lisps,
clackings, mooings, flibbertigibbets of mouth-music.

Everywhere now, till she couldn't forget, till delight,
without clapping its hands, without moving its lips,
turned itself weary, to a tune in her head she couldn't
switch off, a gushing tap stuck at full on. How she
narrowed her eyes at the *Bus Stop*, at *Lyons Maid*,
Little Horse Close, tried to get back to the patterns
as patterns, squinnying hard to unfocus, to skim over
Stop! Children Crossing! Last Day of Sale, over *Entrance*,
No Ball Games, *This Door is Alarmed* and *No Exit*.

The Taxidermist

Most times it's knowing when to stop, to leave it,
to let go's the hardest bit; but this time something
ticks inside his chest. A small flip-flutter
and he's laying down his grooming brush,
standing back to look at hide and flank, at legs
as delicate as wish-bones, those tricky, dainty hooves.

Glossed eyes like alleys shine at him, he knows
their fringes, lash by lash positioned by his steady hand
and sees that it is good, is finished. He folds his arms
across his chest and leans the weight of all his weariness
down through his heels, relieves the slow ache in his back
and sees that this is something other than his making, this

swell and symmetry of belly stripes that shift, as if a breath
is being taken, as if, somewhere inside, a heart is ticking.

Contributors

PAUL BAVISTER teaches creative writing at Oxford University and Birkbeck College, London. He has published three books of poetry, the most recent being *The Prawn Season* (Two Rivers Press, 2002). New work has recently appeared in *The Rialto* and in collaboration with visual artist Beth King.

ADRIAN BLAMIRES studied English at Reading University (1983–1986) and is now back there, studying for an MA in Early Modern Literature and Drama. His career has mainly involved teaching English in sixth form colleges. During the 1990s he attended the Thin Raft poetry workshop at Reading Library. His first collection, *The Effect of Coastal Processes* (Two Rivers Press, 2005) was a Waterstone's Best New Poetry selection and was reviewed in *The Guardian*. Its title poem has been read on Radio 4's *Poetry Please*. His latest collection, *The Pang Valley* (Two Rivers Press, 2010), has been well-received by the Poetry Book Society.

DAVID COOKE was born in 1953 in Wokingham and grew up in Reading. In 1977 his poetry received a Gregory Award. His poems, translations and reviews have been published widely in the UK, Ireland, and mainland Europe. His first collection, *Brueghel's Dancers* (Free Man's Press) was published in 1984. After a long silence he has returned to writing. A new collection, *In The Distance* (Night Publishing), is scheduled for 2011. It will reprint some earlier work alongside a generous sampling of previously uncollected poems. A further collection of more recent pieces, *Work Horses*, is in preparation.

JANE DRAYCOTT'S collections include *Christina the Astonishing* with Lesley Saunders and Peter Hay (Two Rivers Press, 1998), *Prince Rupert's Drop* (OUP/Carcanet, 1999), *Tideway*, illustrated by Peter Hay (Two Rivers Press, 2002), and *The Night Tree* (Carcanet, 2004). She has been nominated for the Forward Prize three times and in 2004 was named as a Next Generation Poet. Her most recent books are *Over* (Carcanet, 2009), shortlisted for the T S Eliot Prize 2009, and a new poetic translation of the medieval dream elegy *Pearl* (Carcanet, 2011). She currently teaches on postgraduate writing courses at Lancaster and Oxford.

CLAIRE DYER writes women's fiction as well as poetry and works part-time for an HR research forum in London. She was short-listed in the 2010 Cinnamon Press Poetry Collection Award, commended in the 2010 Ware Open Poetry Competition and won the 2010 WomenWords poetry competition. She has had poems published by *Orbis*, *Ragged Raven Press*, *Envoi* and *Leaf Books*. Claire regularly reads her poetry at Reading's Poets' Café and, as a member of the Brickwork Poets, performs at venues around the country. She is Chairperson of Reading Writers and recently completed an MA at The University of Reading. Her websites are www.clairedyeronlyconnect.co.uk and www.brickworkpoets.co.uk.

JOHN FROY has lived in Reading and run a decorating business since 1986. He was coordinator and editor at Two Rivers Press from 2003–2010. He has published a first collection of poems, *Eggshell: A Decorator's Notes* (Two Rivers Press, 2007), and a childhood memoir, *70 Waterloo Road* (Pine Wave Press, 2010).

A. F. HARROLD is a poet and performer. Two Rivers Press has published two collections of his poetry, *Logic and the Heart* (2004) and *Flood* (2010), along with a collection of comic verse, *Postcards from the Hedgehog* (2007). His other books include a second collection of comic miscellanea, *The Man who Spent Years in the Bath* (2008), a book of children's poetry, *I Eat Squirrels* (2009), and a novel, *The Education of Epitome Quirkstandard* (2010), all from his cottage industry small press Quirkstandard's Alternative. He is a common sight on stages at literary, poetry and comedy festivals, and runs Reading's monthly poetry night, Poets' Café, at South Street Arts Centre.

IAN HOUSE taught poets from Chaucer to Heaney for over thirty years at schools in Derbyshire, Yorkshire and Reading, and wrote no poems. He took early retirement, taught English in Moscow,

Budapest and Prague, and wrote no poems. When he returned to Reading at the beginning of this millennium, the floodgates opened and he has been scribbling ever since. His first collection is *Cutting the Quick* (Two Rivers Press, 2005).

WENDY KLEIN, born in the USA, is a retired family psychotherapist. She has lived in Sweden, France and Germany, but came to Britain in 1971 and stayed. She has been widely published in magazines and anthologies, and has had many winning and commended poems in UK competitions. Her first collection, *Cuba in the Blood* was published by Cinnamon Press in 2009, and a second, working title *Twenty-two Karat*, is due out late in 2011 or early 2012. She gets her inspiration from travelling to challenging places and from her odd dysfunctional background. Though searching eagerly for new directions, she finds herself repeatedly drawn back to these tantalizing themes.

GILL LEARNER began writing poetry in 2001. Since then her poems have been published in a wide range of journals including *Acumen*, *Poetry News*, *Smiths Knoll* and *Tears in the Fence*. She also has work in a number of anthologies from the following publishers: Blinking Eye, Cinnamon, Grey Hen and Leaf. Her poems have been heard on Radio 3 and BBC *South Today* and won awards such as the Poetry Society's Hamish Canham Prize 2008 and second prize in the Keats-Shelley competition 2010. Her first collection, *The Agister's Experiment* (2011), is published by Two Rivers Press.

KATE NOAKES first came to Reading as an undergraduate in 1980. She has published two collections of poetry: *Ocean to Interior* (Mighty Erudite, 2007) and *The Wall Menders* (Two Rivers Press, 2009). She has performed her poetry at venues as diverse as The Troubadour, The Poetry Society, Glastonbury Festival and on a boat on the Thames at Henley Literary Festival. Her work has been widely published in periodicals and magazines in the UK and beyond.

VICTORIA PUGH was born in London and has lived in Reading for the last twenty-two years. She has an MA in Creative Writing

from Manchester Metropolitan University. She has been successful
or commended in the Cardiff International poetry competition,
Scintilla poetry competition, the Blinking Eye poetry competition
and has been published in various magazines. One of her poems was
highly commended and published in *The Forward Book of Poetry 2009*.
Her first collection, *Mrs Marvellous*, was published by Two Rivers
Press in 2008. She teaches literacy and learning skills at Thames
Valley University.

PETER ROBINSON has published many volumes of poetry, translations,
and literary criticism including *Selected Poems* (Carcanet Press, 2003),
The Look of Goodbye (Shearsman Books, 2008), *English Nettles and
Other Poems* (Two Rivers Press, 2010) and *The Greener Meadow:
Selected Poems of Luciano Erba* (Princeton University Press, 2007),
which won the John Florio Prize. This year, as well as editing
Reading Poetry: an anthology, he has published an edition of Bernard
Spencer's *Complete Poetry, Translations & Selected Prose* (Bloodaxe
Books) and translations of *Poems by Antonia Pozzi* (One World Classics).
He is Professor of English and American Literature at the University
of Reading.

LESLEY SAUNDERS' poetry publications include *Christina the
Astonishing*, with Jane Draycott and artist Peter Hay (Two Rivers Press,
1998), *Her Leafy Eye*, with artist Geoff Carr (Two Rivers Press, 2009),
and most recently *No Doves* (Mulfran Press, 2010). She has recently
held two writing residencies, one in the gardens of Murray Edwards
College, Cambridge, and the other at Acton Court, a Tudor house
near Bristol built for Henry VIII and Anne Boleyn. Lesley was joint
winner, along with Mandy Coe, of the 2008 Manchester Poetry Prize,
and was a finalist in the 2010 competition. She loves collaborations
and impromptu poetry projects.

SUSAN UTTING has won many awards including an Arts Council
Year of the Artist Laureateship, The Berkshire Poetry Prize and
Peterloo Poetry Prize. *Something Small is Missing* (Smith/Doorstop,
1999) was a winner in the Poetry Pamphlet Competition, followed
by her collection *Striptease* (Smith/Doorstop, 2001). *Houses Without*

Walls (Two Rivers Press, 2006) was featured in the *Independent on Sunday* and included in the *Forward Book of Poetry*, Best Single Poem category. New work has recently appeared in the TLS, *The North*, *The Daily Mirror* (Carol Anne Duffy's choice) and was selected by *The Times* for its Best Love Poems 2010 showcase.

JEAN WATKINS began writing poetry in 2002. Her poems have appeared in *Mslexia*, *Magma*, *Boomslang* and *South* (2010) magazines, and in many anthologies including the Reading University Creative Arts Anthology for 2008 and 2009. Some of her poems are available on the *poetry pf* website. She has won third prizes in the Writers' Bureau, Ware, the *Sunday Telegraph* and Havant competitions, and many of her poems have been commended or highly commended. She won the Reading Library competition in 2004, 2008, and 2009, and was placed in 2010. Her poems were shortlisted in the Poetry Business competition for 2008–9.

Two Rivers Press has been publishing in and about Reading since 1994. Founded by the artist Peter Hay (1951–2003), the press continues to delight readers, local and further afield, with its varied list of individually designed, thought-provoking books.